ESSENTIAL
MALTA & GOZO

Original text by Pat Levy and Sean Sheehan
Updated by Lindsay Bennett

© AA Media Limited 2009
First published 2007
Revised 2009

Series Editor Lucy Arthy
Series Designer Sharon Rudd
Cartographic Editor Anna Thompson

ISBN: 978-0-7495-6128-4

Published by AA Publishing, a trading name of AA Media Limited, whose registered office is Fanum House, Basing View, Basingstoke, Hampshire RG21 4EA. Registered number 06112600.

Colour separation: MRM Graphics Ltd
Printed and bound in Italy by Printer Trento S.r.l.

A03804
Maps in this title produced from map data © RMF Publishing and Surveys Ltd (Malta)

About this book

Symbols are used to denote the following categories:

✚ map reference to maps on cover

✉ address or location

☎ telephone number

🕐 opening times

✋ admission charge

🍴 restaurant or café on premises or nearby

Ⓜ nearest underground train station

🚌 nearest bus/tram route

🚉 nearest overground train station

⛴ nearest ferry stop

✈ nearest airport

ℹ tourist information office

❓ other practical information

➤ indicates the page where you will find a fuller description

This book is divided into five sections.

The essence of Malta and Gozo
pages 6–19
Introduction; Features; Food and drink; Short break including the 10 Essentials

Planning pages 20–33
Before you go; Getting there; Getting around; Being there

Best places to see pages 34–55
The unmissable highlights of any visit to Malta and Gozo

Best things to do pages 56–77
Good places to have lunch; top activities; best beaches; places to take the children and more

Exploring pages 78–186
The best places to visit in Malta and Gozo, organized by area

Maps
All map references are to the maps on the covers. For example, Valletta has the reference ✚ K3 – indicating the grid square in which it is to be found.

Admission prices
Inexpensive (under €3)
Moderate (€3–€6)
Expensive (over €6)

Hotel prices
Price are per room per night:
€ budget (under €70)
€€ moderate (€70–€120)
€€€ expensive (over €120)

Restaurant prices
Price for a three-course meal per person without drinks:
€ budget (under €25)
€€ moderate (€25–€35)
€€€ expensive (over €35)

Contents

BEST THINGS TO DO

EXPLORING...

56 – 77

78 – 186

The essence of...

Malta and Gozo draw together a richness of archaeological and architectural treasures, in an hospitable climate where the temperature climbs to 35°C (95°F) and makes the clear sea the most excellent of baths and water sports a pleasure. The islands come to life with festivals known as *festas* which open up Maltese culture to visitors. Even tourist enclaves have their own festivals every night in pubs and discos. The people are Malta's strongest asset. They are proud but not narrowly nationalistic, deeply religious but not repressive, courteous but not superficial. There is an enigma somewhere but it bothers no one.

features

The islands of Malta and Gozo are set right in the middle of the Mediterranean and at the narrowest point, thus smack on an ancient and turbulent crossroads. In striking contrast to their small size, their historical legacy is immense. Once the Romans came for precious honey. Today, as you gaze at honey-coloured walls this sense of age is all-enveloping. The catalogue of fearsome invaders, from ancient times to World War II, has made Malta's language, food and architecture an enticing mix of European, Arabian and British influences. Yet, surprisingly, Malta's culture is distinctively its own.

Here you will find prehistoric monuments built 1,000 years before the pyramids, Roman ruins and the truly awesome defensive works of the Knights of Malta, the latter largely unaltered and part of an extraordinary wealth of architecture. Agriculture and fishing are important, but this is a busy working place with good shopping, numerous markets and a buzzing tourist life.

SIZE

Malta's longest distance from southeast to north-west is 27km (17 miles) and the widest point from east to west is 14km (8.5 miles). Gozo is 14km (8.5 miles) long and 7km (4.5 miles) at its widest.

POPULATION
Some 368,000 Maltese live on the island of Malta and 30,000 live on Gozo (calling themselves Gozitans, not Maltese). Malta ranks fourth in the world in terms of population density.

DIASPORA
An estimated 200,000 Australians are of Maltese origin. Worldwide the figure is put at over 1 million.

LANGUAGES
Maltese and English are the official languages. Italian is widely spoken, German to a lesser extent.

RELIGION
Most Maltese are Roman Catholics.

CULTURAL INFLUENCES
The British influence reveals itself in the colour of the telephone boxes, the popularity of afternoon tea, bacon and eggs for breakfast, and the daily use of English.

The Italian influence is evident in the popularity and prevalence of pasta and pizza dishes. Young people follow Italian trends in fashionable dress, and Italian television channels are broadcast.

The Turkish influence may still be seen in the popularity of Turkish Delight, a jelly-like, sweet dessert. The spectacular walls and bastions of Valletta may also, in one sense, be attributed to the Turks, for they were built to keep them out.

The Arab influence shows itself in the Maltese language, 70 per cent of which is Arabic in origin.

The Catholic influence accounts for the fact that Malta does not have divorce (but does issue annulments of marriage), and abortion is illegal. Local religious festivals erupt with colour and are celebrated all over the island.

food & drink

Hotels and restaurants serve a large range of international cuisines, from Italian to the oriental, with a strong British contribution along the lines of roast beef and apple pie. Less ostentatiously displayed but well worth seeking out are the local establishments which serve the traditional home cooking of the islands.

MALTESE CUISINE

Maltese food owes much to the many cultures of the peoples who have occupied or traded with the island over the centuries. Like Italian food it often uses pasta, and like Moorish food it relies on spicy sauces, but it has a quality of its own which has evolved from the special circumstances of the island. Many vegetables can be grown all year round, while fish tends to be seasonal. The shortage of firewood for ovens in the past meant that food was cooked slowly in earthenware pots or taken to the village baker to be roasted. Despite the advent of modern stoves these styles of cooking are still preferred and they too influence the taste of the food.

Pastry is a common element. Combinations of meat or fish with vegetables and cheeses are

encased in shortcrust or filo-type pastry. A popular dish is the Sicilian *timpana*, a mixture of meat, liver, tomatoes, eggs and pasta with a pastry crust. *Stuffat tal-laham* is a thick, traditional, beef stew made using topside or rump plus whatever vegetables and seasonings are at hand.

Soups are often based on fish with garlic, tomatoes and marjoram. A traditional spring vegetable soup is *kusksu*, made with broad beans, pasta and tomatoes. Look out too for *aljotta*, a fish soup that takes its name from the Italian *aglio* (garlic) which always makes its presence felt in this dish. There is also *soppa ta l-armla*, widow's soup, which uses a mixture of vegetables, tomato paste and eggs, served with cheese and thick slices of local bread.

Traditional meat dishes which should be tried include stewed rabbit cooked in wine and *bragjoli*, little parcels of stuffing wrapped in slices of beef and slowly simmered.

VEGETABLE DISHES

The range of vegetables is extraordinary and because of the traditional abstinence from meat on Fridays many vegetable dishes are available. The Maltese version of ratatouille is called *kapunata*, a mix of garlic, aubergines and peppers. Savoury pumpkin pie is popular, as are spinach and anchovy pies. There is even a Maltese version of minestrone called *minestra* – made with at least eight vegetables – which is often more like a thick vegetable stew than its Italian

counterpart. Accompanied by the excellent Maltese bread, soups make a satisfying meal.

Desserts and sweets are popular, sometimes spectacular, but rarely like the pastries of other European cuisines. On the street, especially during a festival, home-made nougat, iced biscuits stuffed with *figoli* (almond paste) or fresh fruit are sold. Also eaten during festivals is *prinjolata*, a dessert made from a pyramid of sponge fingers, almond cream, chocolate and cherries. Bakeries sell delicious filled pastries, while restaurants offer *helwa tat-Tork*, which is a crushed mix of sugar and almonds.

ALCOHOLIC DRINKS
Local wine is cheap and mostly quite cheerful, but beware of the high alcohol content. Local beers are Hopleaf, and Blue Label and Cisk lager. Lowenbrau and Stella Artois are available. Small cafés usually sell alcohol, and bars sell food and beverages.

short break

If you have only a short time to visit Malta and Gozo and would like to take home some unforgettable memories you can do something local and capture the real flavour of the islands. The following suggestions will give you a wide range of sights and experiences that won't take very long, won't cost very much and will make your visit very special.

- See the *Malta Experience* audio-visual show (➤ 100) in Valletta for an enjoyable dip into history, covering 7,000 years in 50 minutes and set inside the historic Sacra Infermeria (➤ 95). If time and inclination restrict you to visiting just one of the multilingual audio-visual, large-screen presentations about Malta and Gozo, then this is the one to see.

- Go to a *festa,* the Maltese village festival, for the fun and vitality, the colour and the sound effects (➤ 24–25). You certainly can't miss a *festa* week in any Maltese village, with the huge banners, statues of saints and lights galore, brass bands, fast-food sellers, parades and fireworks.

- Enjoy Maltese food by tucking into *pastizzi* (➤ 67) with your mid-morning drink, and have at least one picnic with fresh bread bought before 11am and peppered cheese from Gozo. The Maltese really do have their own cuisine, but you have to seek it out.

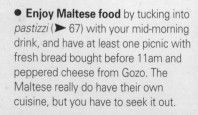

● **Visit St John's Co-Cathedral** in Valletta and see the Caravaggio paintings (➤ 49). The Italian painter came to Malta in 1607 and stayed only 14 months before he escaped from prison for an unknown crime. Be sure to see *The Beheading of St John the Baptist*, his most acclaimed work here.

● **Spend more than a day** in Gozo because the pleasure of being there lies in its unhurried pace and a quick visit will fail to do justice to its many charms (➤ 169–182). Gozo has not been developed to cater for mass tourism, and as a result it is totally different from the island of Malta.

● **See Mdina,** the ancient capital, walled by the Arabs and separated from the suburbs which became Rabat (➤ 118–123). Take a walk (➤ 124–125) as history stares back at you from the walls. This is one of Europe's finest medieval cities and the jewel in Malta's crown.

● **Visit at least one of the prehistoric sites:** The Ħal Saflieni Hypogeum (➤ 42–43) is the most informative. All bear testimony to Colin Renfrew's claim in his book *Before Civilization* that 'the great temples of Malta and Gozo lay claim to be the world's most impressive prehistoric monuments' (➤ 36–37 and 54–55).

● **Go for a walk around Valletta,** visiting a church here, a museum or art gallery there, forts, gardens and the refurbished waterfront (➤ 96). Be prepared for the scale and beauty of Valletta. If you want to understand the history of this remarkable island you simply can't afford to miss this city.

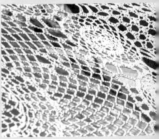

● **Buy some Maltese glass or Maltese lace,** both artistic and affordable examples of Maltese handicrafts. To get a glimpse of how these are produced visit the two craft villages, Ta' Qali on Malta (➤ 152) and Ta' Dbiegi on Gozo.

● **Take a cruise around the Grand Harbour,** a magnificent and truly formidable sight that sparks the imagination (➤ 154). This is the biggest and one of the most dramatic harbours in the Mediterranean, and is steeped in history. The huge fortifications around Valletta are quite a sight.

Planning

Before you go

WHEN TO GO

JAN	FEB	MAR	APR	MAY	JUN	JUL	AUG	SEP	OCT	NOV	DEC
15°C	15°C	16°C	19°C	23°C	28°C	30°C	31°C	28°C	24°C	20°C	17°C
59°F	59°F	61°F	66°F	73°F	82°F	86°F	88°F	82°F	75°F	68°F	63°F

🌧️ 🌦️ ☀️ 🌦️ ☀️ ☀️ ☀️ ☀️ ☀️ ☀️ 🌧️ 🌧️

● High season   ● Low season

Temperatures are the average daily maximum for each month. Average daily minimum temperatures are 5° to 9°C (9° to 16°F) lower. The best times of the year for good weather are May, June and early to mid-September, when it is warm and dry without being uncomfortably hot. July and August are scorching, with temperatures pushing up to the mid-30s°C (90s°F).

On the coast sea breezes usually make life more bearable, though the hot dry sirocco can sweep in from North Africa and make things worse. High winds sometimes occur during spring and there is heavy rainfall, often in October, and between then and March showers are likely. Little rain falls in May, June and August and virtually none in July.

WHAT YOU NEED

		UK	Germany	USA	Netherlands	Spain
● Required	Some countries require a passport to remain valid for a minimum period (usually at least six months) beyond the date of entry – contact their consulate or embassy or your travel agent for details.					
○ Suggested						
▲ Not required						
Passport (or National Identity Card where applicable)		●	●	●	●	●
Visa (regulations can change – check before you travel)		▲	▲	▲	▲	▲
Onward or Return Ticket		●	●	●	●	●
Health Inoculations (tetanus and polio)		▲	▲	▲	▲	▲
Health Documentation (► 23, Health Insurance)		●	●	●	●	●
Travel Insurance		○	○	○	○	○
Driving Licence (national)		●	●	●	●	●
Car Insurance Certificate		●	●	●	●	●
Car Registration Document		●	●	●	●	●

WEBSITES

National Tourist Board of Malta:
www.visitmalta.com
www.malta.com
www.gov.mt

www.maltavista.net
www.maltalinks.com
www.malta.co.uk
www.yourmalta.com

TOURIST OFFICES AT HOME

In the UK

(also responsible for Eire)
Malta Tourist Office
☒ Unit C Parkhouse
14 Northfields
London SW18 1DD
☎ 020 8877 6991;
www.visitmalta.com

In Malta

(responsible for USA and Canada)
Malta Tourism Authority
☒ Auberge D'Italie
Merchants Street
Valletta VLT 1170
☎ 21237349 (customer care line)

HEALTH INSURANCE

Nationals of other EU countries can get medical treatment in state
hospitals on production of the European Health Insurance Card (EHIC).
This can be obtained from the Department of Health in the UK
(tel: 020 7210 4850; www.dh.gov.uk), though private medical health
insurance is still advised and is essential for all other visitors.

Dental treatment must be paid for. If you need a dentist enquire at the
hotel reception desk or call directory enquiries (tel: 1182). Private medical
insurance covers dental treatment and is advised for all visitors.

TIME DIFFERENCES

GMT	Malta	Germany	USA (NY)	Netherlands	Spain
12 noon	1PM	1PM	7AM	1PM	1PM

Malta is one hour ahead of Greenwich Mean Time (GMT+1), but from
late March, when clocks are put forward one hour, to late September,
summer time (GMT+2) operates.

NATIONAL HOLIDAYS

1 January *New Year's Day*

10 February *Feast of St Paul's Shipwreck*

19 March *Feast of St Joseph*

31 March *Freedom Day*

March/April *Good Friday*

1 May *Workers' Day*

7 June *Sette Giugno*

(Commemoration of 7 June 1919)

29 June *Feast of St Peter and St Paul*

15 August *Feast of the Assumption*

8 September *Victory Day*

21 September *Independence Day*

8 December *Feast of the Immaculate Conception*

13 December *Republic Day*

25 December *Christmas Day*

Most shops, offices and museums close on these days.

WHAT'S ON WHEN

Between May and October every town and village celebrates the feast day *(festa)* of its patron saint.

1 Jan New Year's Day

10 Feb Feast of St Paul's Shipwreck, Valletta

31 Mar Freedom Day

Holy Week Good Friday processions are held in various villages and

towns around Malta and Gozo on the afternoon of Good Friday, a public holiday. Good Friday pageants are held in 14 different towns and villages, featuring a number of life-sized statues depicting religious scenes. There will also be men and women in period costume personifying biblical characters. Many places of entertainment are closed but cinemas and cafés remain open on Good Friday.

1 May Worker's Day

7 Jun Sette Giugno (commemorating 7 June 1919)

29 Jun Feast of St Peter and Paul. Parish *festa* in Nadur (Gozo)

15 Aug Feast of the Assumption. Parish festas in Attard, Għaxaq, Gudja,

Mġarr, Mosta, Mqabba, Qrendi, Victoria Cathedral (Gozo)
8 Sep Victory Day
21 Sep Independence Day
8 Dec Feast of the Immaculate Conception
13 Dec Republic Day
25 Dec Christmas Day

Other parish *festas* in Malta
Tel: 21241281 for information.
Balluta Last Sun in Jul
Balzan 2nd Sun in Jul
Birkirkara 1st Sun in Jul, 3rd or 4th Sun in Aug
Birżebbuġa 1st Sun in Aug
Dingli 3rd Sun in Aug
Floriana 3rd Sun after Easter
Għargħur 24 Aug or the Sun after
Gzira 2nd Sun in Jul
Marsaskala 26 Jul or the Sun after
Marsaxlokk 1st Sun in Aug
Mdina Last Sun in Jan
Qormi Last Sun in Jun and 3rd Sun in Jul
Rabat 1st Sun in Jul
Sliema 2nd Fri of Lent, 1st and 3rd Sun in Jul, the Sun after 18 Aug and 1st Sun in Sep
St Julian's Last Sun in Aug
St Paul's Bay Last Sun in Jul
Valletta 3rd Sun after Easter, 1st Sunday before 4 Aug
Vittoriosa 10 Aug or nearest Sun
Żurrieq 1st Sun in Sep

Other parish *festas* in Gozo
Għarb 1st Sun in Jul
San Lawrenz 2nd Sun in Aug
Sannat 4th Sun in Jul
Victoria 3rd Sun in Jul
Xewkija 4th Sun in Jun
Żebbuġ 4th Sun in Aug

Getting there

BY AIR

Malta (Luqa) Airport

8km (5 miles) from city centre

 N/A

 50 minutes

 35 minutes

Grand Harbour (Valletta)

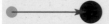

1km (0.6 miles) from city centre

N/A

N/A

2 minutes

The national airline, Air Malta (tel: 21662211; www.airmalta.com), operates scheduled flights from major European cities; there are also charter flights. Gozo has no airport. Embarkation cards to be filled in before passport control. There are no direct scheduled flights to Malta from the USA, Canada, Australia or New Zealand. Transatlantic fly to a European hub airport (for example London or Rome) and then on to Malta.

Arriving by air Malta International Airport, at Luqa, is the archipelago's only international terminal. It lies 8km (5 miles) from Valletta, 13km (8 miles) from St Julian's, 22km (14 miles) from Mellieħa and 8km (5 miles) from Marsaskala. Outside rush hour nowhere on the island is more than a 30- to 45-minute drive from the airport. For airport enquiries call 21249600 or click on www.maltairport.com.

Getting to Valletta from the airport Valletta is a 20- to 30-minute ride on bus No 8. The bus runs Mon–Fri 6am–9pm and Sat–Sun 6am–9:30pm.

From the Valletta terminus you can get a bus to anywhere on the island. If you want to go somewhere other than Valletta from the airport, you will have to get a taxi or rent a car.

Taxis from the airport Fares from the airport are regulated and prepaid tickets can be purchased in the arrivals hall. Pick up a sheet of fares from the tourist office in Arrivals for your destination and note that the price covers up to four persons 'with normal sized luggage' at any time of day. To pre-book a taxi call Wembleys, tel: 21374141; www.wembleys.net.

Getting from Malta to Gozo Most tour operators include onward transport to Gozo from Malta, but if you are travelling independently there are two options. The vast majority of people cross the Gozo Channel by ferry from Ċirkewwa (at the northern tip of Malta) to Mġarr on Gozo. The service runs every half an hour or so through the day and less frequently through the night. From July to September it runs 24 hours, from October to June it runs from 5am to 11pm. The journey takes 25–30 minutes and also transports vehicles. It is very cheap for pedestrians and inexpensive for drivers, too. Confusingly there is no ticket for the journey going out to Gozo, but you must buy a return ticket at the kiosk at Mġarr harbour before boarding for the return trip; Gozo Channel also run a direct bus service from Malta Airport to the ferry at Ċirkewwa. Services run at least five times per day in peak season. Tickets can be pre-booked or bought on the bus, tel: 21556114 (Mġarr); 21580435 (Ċirkewwa); www.gozochannel.com. There is also a ferry service from Sa Maison (Msida, near Valletta) to Mġarr on Gozo which takes 1 hour 15 minutes and sails three times per week (Mon, Tue, Thu) in peak season; call ahead for timetable, tel: 21561622 or 21556114. On Gozo the Mġarr to Victoria bus schedule follows the ferry timetable so that connections link up.

Getting from Malta to Comino Crossings for Hotel Comino residents are arranged by the island's one and only hotel. Pleasure boats from all over Gozo and Malta also visit Comino on day trips. Contact the tourist information office for details.

BY SEA

There are ferry and catamaran services from southern Italy and Sicily to Malta (Valletta). A frequent ferry service operates from Malta to Gozo (Mġarr) departing from Ċirkewwa (20-minute crossing). A ferry service also operates from Sa Maison (75 minutes). For information on all services, see above.

Getting around

Seaplane The quickest way to travel between Malta and Gozo is by seaplane from Valletta harbour to Mġarr harbour. Contact Harbourair on 21228302; www.harbourairmalta.com.

Cross island buses Most of Malta's towns and villages are connected to Valletta by bus. Fares range from €0.47 to €1.16. Usually they depart from and return to City Gate (the main terminus). Buses (yellow with an orange stripe) are numbered but their destination is not shown. However, billboards showing the destination and route number can be found in the City Gate Bus Terminus and the tourist office dispenses a free bus map.

On Gozo, buses (grey with a red stripe) serve the main villages from Victoria but only run in the morning. Bus passes for 1, 3, 5 and 7 days may be purchased at the Valletta or Buġibba terminals or the Sliema ferry terminal, tel: 21250007; www.atp.com.mt.

Ferries Ferries from Malta to Gozo (Mġarr) depart from Ċirkewwa (20-minute crossing) or Sa Maison (75 minutes). Services are frequent. In summer there are also passenger-only hover-marine services from Sa Maison to Mġarr (25 minutes) and from Sliema (30 minutes); some trips go via the island of Comino. For information on all services tel: 21243964/5/6.

Urban transport Valletta is the only major conurbation on Malta, but as driving is virtually impossible around the city most people walk. From the main bus terminus at City Gate buses are destined for other parts of the island, except for bus 98, which follows a circular route around Valletta, and is probably your best bet.

TAXIS

Mostly white Mercedes with distinctive 'taxi' sign on roof. They do not cruise but can be picked up at the airport, hotels, harbours and central ranks or by phone. Black taxis also operate, at cheaper rates, but need to be booked by phone. Wembleys, tel: 21374141.

DRIVING

- There are no motorways on Malta or Gozo. Drive on the left.
- Speed limits on country roads: 80kph/49mph
  Speed limits in built-up areas: 50kph/31mph
- Seat belts must be worn in front seats at all times.
- Random breath-testing. Never drive under the influence of alcohol.
- Petrol (super grade and unleaded) is readily available. Service stations open 7am–6pm (4pm Saturday); some to 7pm in summer. On Sundays and public holidays a few stations open on a rota basis 8am–noon, so make sure you have enough fuel on Saturday night if planning an excursion. Petrol stations do not accept cheques or credit cards.
- If you are involved in a road traffic accident, call the police immediately (tel: 112), and do not move the vehicle as it may invalidate your insurance. In the event of a breakdown there are two breakdown companies: RMF (tel: 2124222 Malta; 21558844 Gozo) and MTC (tel: 2143333). If you break down in a rented car, call the rental company to request help.

CAR RENTAL

Rates vary, but as mileage and insurance is included, it is cheap for Europe. Avis (tel: 25677550; www.avis.com), Europcar (tel: 25761000; www.europcar.com.mt) and Hertz (tel: 21314626; www.hertz.com) accept credit cards. Signposting is poor and so is the quality of the roads.

FARES AND TICKETS

Public buses offer passes giving unlimited travel for 1, 3, 5, or 7 days. These work out cheaper if you take several journeys per day, and can be purchased from the driver, or at ATP ticket booths and machines. Remember that not all attractions have good public transport links and journeys may involve connecting routes.

Many attractions in Malta offer discounted fares for children, students and senior citizens. Rules on exact age varies and it's important to carry proof of age if you want to claim the discount. Government museums also offer discounts to ISIC and Euro<26 cardholders.

Being there

TOURIST OFFICES
Malta – Head Office
National Tourism Organization, Auberge D'Italie, Merchants Street, Valletta ☎ 22915000; www.visitmalta.com
Local Tourist Information Offices
● Malta, 1 City Arcades, Valletta

☎ 21237747
● Malta (Luqa) International Airport, Arrivals Hall, Gudja ☎ 23696073
● Gozo, Tigrija Palazz, Republic Street, Victoria (Rabat)
☎ 21561419

MONEY
The monetary unit of Malta is the euro (€) which replaced the Maltese lira in January 2008. The euro is divided into 100 cents. Coins come in denominations of 1, 2, 5, 10, 20 and 50 cents, 1 euro and 2 euros. Notes come in denominations of 5, 10, 20, 50, 100, 200 and 500 euros.

POSTAL AND INTERNET SERVICES
There are post offices in most towns and villages. The main post offices are in Valletta at Dar i-Annona, Misrah Kastilja, open Mon–Fri 7:15–11, 12:30–4, and 129 Republic Street, Victoria (Gozo), open Mon–Fri 8:15am–4:30pm, Sat 8:15am–12.30pm. Otherwise hours are: Mon–Sat 7:30–12:45, closed Sun. Tel: freephone 800 7 22 44; www.maltapost.com.

TIPS/GRATUITIES

Yes ✓   No ✗

Restaurants (if service not included)	✓	10%
Cafés/bars	✓	change
Taxis	✗	
Porters	✓	€1–€2
Chambermaids	✓	€1–€2
Cloakroom attendants	✓	change
Hairdressers	✓	10%
Theatre/cinema usherettes	✓	small change
Toilets	✓	small change

Malta is well supplied with internet cafés and there is usually one in every major town or resort. Many hotels have guest internet access through a dedicated machine on site and five-star hotels will have internet connection in the rooms (though there may be an extra charge). WiFi connection hotspots are growing in number but are mainly found in the lobbies of major hotels.

TELEPHONES

Malta's public telephone boxes are either green, red or see-through booths. Few phones accept coins but most take a phonecard *(telecard)* available in denominations of €5, €10 and €15 from Telemalta offices, post offices, banks and newsagents.

All telephone numbers in Malta and Gozo are 8-figure and there is no area code.

Emergency telephone numbers

Police 112

Fire 199 (in Gozo 21562044)

Ambulance 196

Air rescue 21244371

Sea rescue 21238797

International dialling codes

From Malta to:

UK 00 44

Germany 00 49

USA 00 1

Netherlands 00 31

Spain 00 34

EMBASSIES AND CONSULATES

UK ☎ 23230000 (High Commission)

Germany ☎ 21336520 (Embassy)

USA ☎ 2561400; 25614000 (Embassy)

ELECTRICITY

The local power supply is 220/240 volts, 50Hz. Sockets take square plugs with 3 square pins (as used in the UK). Visitors from continental Europe should bring an adaptor, US visitors a voltage transformer.

HEALTH AND SAFETY

Sun advice The Maltese Islands have virtually year-round sunshine. Wear a sunhat when the sun is at its strongest, and covering up the skin is recommended. No topless or nude sunbathing is allowed.

Drugs In Malta, pharmacies, usually known as chemists, are recognizable by a neon green cross sign. They sell most international medicines over the counter or by prescription.

Safe water Tap water is quite safe though not very palatable. Water from fountains should be avoided as it may not come directly from the mains supply. Bottled 'table' water is available everywhere at a reasonable cost.

Personal safety The crime rate in Malta is low. The police *(pulizija)* – blue uniforms similar to British police – have a station in every town and village. Report any crime to them immediately.

Take sensible precautions to avoid crime:

● Leave valuables in the hotel or apartment safe, not on the beach.
● Don't make yourself an obvious target for bag-snatchers or pickpockets.
● Don't leave valuables visible in a car.

OPENING HOURS

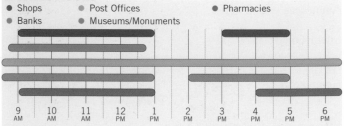

● Shops ● Post Offices ● Pharmacies
● Banks ● Museums/Monuments

9 AM   10 AM   11 AM   12 PM   1 PM   2 PM   3 PM   4 PM   5 PM   6 PM

In addition to the times shown above, many shops in tourist areas stay open throughout the day. In Valletta shops close at 1pm Sat, and except for a few in Buġibba, shops are closed Sun. Banks are open Mon–Fri 8:30–12:30, Sat 8:30–11:30, though foreign exchange is available at many bank branches Mon–Fri until 4pm. ATMs taking international cards can be found in all major towns and resort areas. Banks, shops and museums are closed on national holidays. Restaurants and bars remain open.

LANGUAGE

Maltese and English are the official languages of Malta and Gozo. Almost everyone speaks English but it is Maltese that is normally heard on the streets and that predominates in the media. Maltese comprises a vast element of words of Italian, French and English origin. Menus are all in English but road signs are for the most part in Maltese. Below is a list of a few words that may be helpful.

hello	*merħba*	help!	*ajjut!*
goodbye	*saħħa*	today	*illum*
goodnight	*bonswa*	tomorrow	*għada*
yes	*iva*	yesterday	*il-bieraħ*
no	*le*	how much?	*kemm?*
please	*jekk jogħġbok*	expensive	*għoli*
thank you	*grazzi*	open	*miftuħ*
sorry	*jiddispjaċini*	closed	*magħluq*
bank	*bank*	pound sterling	*lira sterlina*
exchange office	*uffiċju tal-kambju*	banknote	*karta tal-flus*
post office	*posta*	coin	*munita*
cashier	*kaxxier*	credit card	*karta ta' kredtu*
foreign exchange	*uffiċju tal-kambju*	exchange rate	*rata tal-kambju*
foreign currency	*flus barranin*	commission charge	*senserija*
restaurant	*rèstorant*	starter	*starter*
café	*café*	main course	*ikla*
table	*mejda*	dessert	*deserta*
menu	*menu*	drink	*xorb*
lunch	*kolazjonn*	waiter	*waiter*
dinner	*jantar*	the bill	*kont*
aeroplane	*ajruplan*	ferry	*vapur*
airport	*ajruport*	..terminal	*terminal*
bus	*karozza tal-linja*	ticket	*biljett*
..station	*stazzjon tal karozza tal-linja*	..single/return...	*singlu/bir-ritorn*
		ticket office	*uffiċju tal biljetti*
railway station	*stazzjon tal ferrovija*	timetable	*orarju*

Best places to see

1 Ġgantija Temples

Immense bare rock, curious features and primitive attempts at decoration are the stunning signs of this 5,000-year-old technology and culture.

Dating back to 3500–3000BC, Malta's 'Copper Age', the temples at Ġgantija (pronounced *Jagan-Teeya*) on Gozo are thought to be the oldest free-standing monuments in the world. The site is an artificial plateau with a sweeping panorama. Primitive in structure, it is its size which creates a sense of wonder, particularly the outer walls. According to legend, they were built by a female giant. The coralline limestone blocks which make up the outer wall, some weighing as much as 20 tonnes, were quarried from the hill on the other side of the valley and probably rolled and dragged over using the rounded stones that lie scattered around the front of the temples as rollers. The blocks were stood upright by building earth ramps, and large vertical supporting slabs support smaller rectangular blocks.

The temples themselves tell us something about the organization and religion of the complex society that built these structures. Two buildings, one

larger and older than the other, seem to have been places of worship dedicated to a fertility goddess. It has even been suggested that the shape of the structures themselves represent the body of the goddess (head and breasts).

Inside the smaller structure, about 200 years later in origin, stone female figures were found, although these belong to a later date than the construction of the buildings. In the doorway of the larger structure are hinge holes used to support doors which would once have separated the worshippers from the priests, who were in the outer and central inner temples. Inside, two holes in the floor are thought to be libation holes, where the blood of the sacrificed was poured. In the centre of the building, which was once 6m (20ft) high with a domed roof, a large triangular stone and another one carved into the shape of a phallus were found.

✚ *Gozo d2* ✉ Ġgantija, near Xagħra, Gozo ☎ 21553194 ⏰ Daily 9–5 ✋ Moderate 🍽 Oleander (€€), Victory Square, Xagħra (☎ 21557230) 🚌 64, 65 from Victoria

2 Grand Harbour

Spread out like a living painting, several hundred years of history bake quietly in the Mediterranean sunshine.

The truly formidable ramparts are best viewed from one of the many boats which go out into the harbour for a day or half-day trip. However there are several good viewing points from land, particularly from Upper Barrakka Gardens (➤ 96). Boat tours generally leave from **Sliema Marina** passing Fort Manoel on the right and crossing Marsamxett Harbour, where the northern fortifications of Valletta can be seen. Grand Harbour itself is guarded by the two forts of Fort St Elmo (➤ 90) and Fort Ricasoli. As you pass Fort St Elmo you can see damage done by the Italians in 1941.

Built as a fortress city and developed as a naval base and dockyard by the British, Valletta sits snugly between this harbour and Marsamxett. Looking up at the towering eastern shore of Valletta the wharves of the marina, with its 16th- and 17th-century buildings, can be seen, surmounted by the Sacra Infermeria (➤ 95), Lower Barrakka Gardens and Upper Barrakka Gardens. Opposite Valletta's eastern defences are the fingers of land which make up Senglea and Vittoriosa. Between them can be seen the Cottonera Lines, a great 2km (1.2-mile) inland defensive wall built in the 1670s. In 1565 the Knights of St John strung a chain between the tips of these two

points to prevent the Turkish fleet of 200 vessels from entering Dockyard Creek, which was then the main harbour. Dominating the whole scene is Fort St Angelo (► 128–129), while the new cruise port in the shadow of Valletta welcomes the Mediterranean's largest and most modern vessels.

✚ K3

Sliema Marina

🕒 Tours leave from Sliema Marina, check times 🍴 Lunch and dinner cruises are available 🚌 60, 61, 62, 63, 64, 67, 68 from Valletta; 70 from Buġibba; 65 from Rabat; 645 from Ċirkewwa; 652 from Golden Bay

ℹ️ Valletta–Sliema ferry (☎ 2346333, 23463333)

3 Ħaġar Qim and Mnajdra

Over a thousand years before the pyramids, two temples were built on an evocative and spectacular site close to the sea.

The two temple complexes illustrate the ingenuity and intricate social structure of a society that lived here for 3,000 years, then suddenly disappeared between 2500 and 1800BC. This is megalithic architecture of a high order.

Ħaġar Qim ('Standing Stones'), first excavated in 1839, is a series of radiating oval rooms added on at various times to a trefoil structure. Holes around the entrance show where hinged doors once stood with bars to lock them shut. The stone is soft globigerina limestone, which was easy to decorate, as can be seen in the pitted and spiral decoration, which accordingly has weathered badly. One stone here measures 7m by 3m (23ft by 10ft).

Mnajdra, the second temple site, is a five-minute walk away in the direction of the sea but in a more sheltered spot. Made from a harder coralline limestone, it is far better preserved. The three temples share a common outer wall and presumably at one time shared a roof. There are the same patterns of pitted and spiral decorations, an outer temple with inner sanctuaries, carved recesses, trilithion door frames (two large pillars holding up a third block) and, in the second temple, an oracular window (through which the high priest or oracle might have spoken).

Both Ħaġar Qim and Mnajdra are thought to be expressions of a fertility-worshipping religion. Carved obese female figures have been found at both sites, as well as numerous other artefacts which can be seen in the National Museum of Archaeology in Valletta (➤ 93).

The small islet to be seen out at sea is Filfla, just 1km (0.5 miles) in circumference.

➕ G5 ✉ 1.5km (1 mile) southwest of Qrendi ☎ 21424231 🕐 Daily 9–5 (for both temples) 👣 Moderate 🍴 Bar and restaurant (€€) near the car park 🚌 38, 138 ❓ It is planned to open the Mnajdra temple in time to experience the sunrise on the spring equinox. This is to become an annual event, but contact the tourist office beforehand

4 Ħal Saflieni Hypogeum

This vast and complex underground carved temple with catacombs is unique in Malta and in Europe.

This underground burial place and temple was discovered in 1902 by workmen, who were laying the foundations of a house when they broke through the roof of the upper temple. Realizing that building would stop if the authorities discovered its existence, they kept quiet, but three years later the news was out. The site was excavated and found to consist of three levels of catacombs, descending to 11m (36ft), the highest and oldest level being naturally occurring chambers while the two lower levels were carved out of the soft limestone.

After a lengthy period of renovation, the Hypogeum is again open to the public. A visit begins with a video show that places the Hypogeum in its historical context, followed by a guided tour of the three levels. The tour provides a lot of information and questions can be asked along the way but, as the guide will tell you, there is a lot of educated conjecture when it comes to explaining the Hypogeum. The top level was in use *c*3000BC as a burial ground. Descending by modern stairs to the mid level, visitors encounter carved pillars as well as spiral and hexagonal decorations, probably created around 2500BC. The guide gives a possible explanation for the Oracle Chamber and points out parts of the walls still bearing traces of the red ochre once used as decoration. Visitors can see but not step down into the lowest level.

Besides human remains, statues, amulets, vases and other objects were found during excavation. Replicas of many of these can be seen in the exhibition area at the Hypogeum; the originals are in the National Museum of Archaeology in Valleta (➤ 93).

✚ J4 ✉ Burials Street, Paola ☎ 21805018 🕓 Daily 9–4. Tours on the hour, except noon ✋ Expensive 🍴 Cafés and restaurants in Paola (€) 🚌 8, 11 ❓ Tour tickets should be purchased in advance. Booking a week ahead can be necessary at busy times as a maximum of 10 people is allowed per group. Tickets are available from the site itself, the National Museum of Archaeology on Malta; Ġgantija Temples and the Museum of Archaeology on Gozo

5 National Museum of Fine Arts

Enter the welcome cool and elegant interior of the building to find a minor treasure house of Western European art.

This notable building dates back to the 16th century,

when it was the palace of a French knight. Famous figures inhabiting it over the centuries include Charles d'Orleans, brother of King Louis Philippe of France, who died here. For a time it was the British Admiralty House, but was returned to Maltese ownership in 1964; it became the home of the museum in 1974. The whole style of the building, including the magnificent staircase with

two flights of semicircular steps, contributes a sense of serenity and elegance to what is a noted collection of art. On three floors there are 30 rooms full of remarkable paintings.

On the first floor, over a dozen rooms display paintings from the 14th to 17th centuries representing Venetian, Dutch and Italian schools. Plaster models by the local artist Sciortino can be found here also. The great Calabrian baroque artist Mattia Preti is well represented in rooms 12 and 13 with works such as The Martyrdom of St Catherine, while room 14 has paintings by Antoine de Favray and is known as Favray's Room. In room 4 are paintings by Domenico Tintoretto (a relative of the famous Tintoretto), Palma il Giovane and Andrea Vincentino.

Rooms 20 to 23 are dedicated to works by 17th- to 20th-century Maltese artists. The museum also contains a particularly fine array of antique Maltese furniture. A display of relics from the era of the Knights may reopen in the basement of the museum at a later date.

🖽 *Valletta b3* ✉ South Street, Valletta ☎ 21225769
🕐 Daily 9–5 ✋ Inexpensive 🍴 Scalini restaurant opposite (➤ 98)

6 Palace of the Grandmasters

The official residence of the Grandmasters until 1798 is now home to Malta's Parliament.

The Palace was originally a great house built for a Grandmaster's nephew in 1569. It was extended two years later by Gerolamo Cassar into a two-storey building enclosing two courtyards: Neptune Court, with its central bronze statue of Neptune, and Prince Alfred Court, each entered by a separate doorway in the rather plain facade. In Prince Alfred's Court note the Pinto Clock Tower with its mechanical figures, erected in 1745.

Inside, many of the State apartments are decorated with friezes depicting episodes from the history of the Order. There are portraits of the Grandmasters and of European monarchs, interesting furniture and works of art. In the Small Council Chamber are particularly beautiful 18th-century Gobelin tapestries. In the Hall of St Michael and St George, once the throne room, are paintings, notably a frieze showing the Great Siege by Mateo Perez d'Aleccio, a pupil of Michaelangelo. The Hall of Ambassadors is hung with red damask, paintings and another d'Aleccio frieze. The Yellow State Room, once the room where the Grandmaster's retinue of pages lived, has paintings by Batoni and Ribera.

Prince Albert's Court leads to the Armoury, a converted stables, which for those with children will be the most interesting part of the visit. Here you'll see hundreds of exhibits of armour, weaponry and ordnance date back to the siege of 1565. Looking at the armour you understand why the circular steps leading up to the main building are so shallow: one suit weighed as much as 50kg (110 pounds), making it difficult for a knight in full armour to climb them.

✚ *Valletta e3* ✉ Palace Square, Republic Street, Valletta
☎ 21221221 🕐 Mon–Fri 9:30–4:30, Sat 9:30–12:20
🍴 Moderate 🍴 Blue Room (➤ 97) ❓ The Palace is
closed to visitors when Parliament is sitting

7 St John's Co-Cathedral and Museum

Its austere, 16th-century exterior belies the stunning baroque interior, where the magnificence and wealth of the Order is evident in works of art.

Built in the 16th century, this was, until 1798, the Conventual Church of the Order of the Knights of St John. The wide plain facade with the two bell towers of the Co-Cathedral ('Co-' because there are two cathedrals) seems dull. Once inside though, there is almost too much to take in.

The interior, once as austere as its exterior, was redesigned in the baroque style. A central nave has side chapels, each dedicated to a different *langue* of the Order. On the barrel-vaulted ceiling is a series of oil-on-plaster paintings by Mattia Preti showing 18 episodes in the life of St John the Baptist. The floor is paved with the ornate and highly individual multicoloured marble tombstones of Knights.

At the left of the main door is the Chapel of Germany, dedicated to the Epiphany. Through the narrow ambulatory is the Chapel of Italy, which once held Caravaggio's painting *St Jerome* (now in the cathedral museum). Next, the Chapel of France has an altarpiece by Preti. The Chapel of Provence has a painting of St Michael above the altar. Beyond it is the Chapel of the Holy Relics, looted by Napoleon in 1798. Above the crypt, usually closed to the public, is the marble, lapis lazuli and bronze altar. The huge marble group in the apse by Giuseppe Mazzuoli depicts the baptism of Christ.

The Chapel of Auvergne has three works by Giuseppe d'Arena, while the Chapel of Aragon contains the first piece of work done by Preti for the Knights: *St George and the Dragon*. Beyond the entrance to the Oratory the last chapel is that of Castille et Leon, dedicated to St James.

The oratory and museum contain two Caravaggio paintings, *St Jerome* and *The Beheading of St John the Baptist*, the latter being his only signed work and considered a masterpiece.

✚ *Valletta d4* ✉ St John's Square, Valletta ☎ 21220536
🕐 Mon–Fri 9:30–4:30, Sat 9:30–12:30. Closed public hols
✋ Moderate

8 St Paul's and St Agatha's Catacombs

Wander among 3sq km (1.1sq miles) of dimly lit, claustrophobic and eerily empty tombs under the ancient town of Rabat.

St Paul's Catacombs, the largest of Rabat's catacomb complexes, is a labyrinth of corridors and burial chambers. Although plundered many years ago, the empty graves are found in three basic styles. The canopied grave is a little like a four-poster bed, with a flat slab overhung with a

canopy cut from the soft limestone rock. Another type is the saddest: the *loculus*, a tiny rectangular recess cut into the wall to hold the grave of a child. Others, called floor graves, are cut into the floor and would have been covered with a slab of rock. A thousand corpses must once have rested here. Scattered around the graves are roughly hewn tables with circular benches around them. They were probably used by the families of the recently entombed for a religious service after the burial, or on anniversaries.

Close by, St Agatha's catacombs, below the church, are so named because the saint is said to

have lived here for a while to escape the attentions of the Emperor Decius. Fewer catacombs are visited on the 30-minute tour, but there are over 30 frescoes dating back to the 12th to 15th centuries, depicting St Agatha and other Christian figures. Here is the *arcosolium* type of tomb: arched windows cut into the rock wall. In the convent beside St Agatha's Church is a museum with related and unrelated exhibits, and outside is a good green area where you can rest to recover from the gloom and low ceilings.

✚ F3 ✉ Triq Sant'Agata, Rabat ☎ 21454562 (St Paul's), 21454503 (St Agatha's) ⏱ Daily 9–5. Closed public hols ✋ Inexpensive 🍴 Cafés and restaurants (€) nearby 🚌 80, 81, 84 from Valletta; 86 from Buġibba; 65 from Sliema

9 St Paul's Cathedral

An ancient cathedral that is a masterpiece as well as a treasure chamber of Maltese baroque art.

The belfries and dome – probably the finest on Malta – dominate the skyline, and the frontal exterior, with three balanced bays separated by Corinthian pillars, has an altogether grander presence than that of St John's Co-Cathedral in Valletta. This is the finest of Lorenzo Gafà's churches, built between 1697 and 1702. However, the interior, in the form of a Latin cross, may seem gloomy despite the profusion of reds and golds. There are numerous frescoes by Mattia Preti showing events in the life of St Paul, including the saint's appearance on a white horse when the city was besieged by Saracens in 1442. The vaulted ceiling is covered in more frescoes by Vincenzo and Antonio Manno. The carved Irish bog-oak doors to the sacristy were once part of the original church, which was destroyed in the bad earthquake of 1693. The

floor is covered in the funerary slabs of church and local dignitaries. In the Chapel of the Blessed Sacrament is a 12th-century icon of the Madonna and Child. The marble font is from the 15th century, and the marquetry stalls date from 1481.

The museum stands on an ancient site, thought to be the villa of Publius, the Roman governor who was converted to Christianity by St Paul. The collection of artwork donated in 1833 includes works by Dürer and Goya, while later donations include *St John the Baptist* by Ferretti and The *Adoration of the Shepherds* by Subleyras. There are vestments of ancient lace, manuscripts and collections of silver and coins. The ground floor has a collection of Punic and Roman items, while the corridor contains the original panels from the 14th-century choir stalls of the cathedral.

✚ F3 ✉ St Paul's Square, Mdina
☎ 21454136 (cathedral), 21454697 (museum)
🕐 Mon–Sat 9–4:30, Sun open only for Mass
🖐 Inexpensive 🍴 Cafés and restaurants nearby (➤ 148–149) 🚌 80, 86 from Valletta; 65 from Sliema ❓ Festival of Conversion of St Paul, 25 Jan. Festival of St Peter and St Paul, 29 Jun. Pontifical Masses on Church festivals. No admittance to non-devotees during church services

10 Tarxien Temples

The largest of the prehistoric remains was a rich depository of art, created by temple builders, and in striking contrast to the nearby Hypogeum.

The oldest of the three temples in this complex is some 6,000 years old, while the other two were built at later stages. The South Temple, the first temple you come to, was the second to have been built. It has a central paved square surrounded by carved stone benches and a ritual fire was probably lit in the centre of this area. There is a stone basin and an altar, both used in the ceremonies that took place. Many remains were found here, including burned bones of animals, which are represented on the frieze around the next chamber's walls.

The most imposing of the buildings, the Central Temple, was the last to be built (c2400BC), at the peak of the Tarxien period. It too has a central paved area with a hearth for sacrificial fires. One of the side rooms contains a huge bowl carved from a single piece of stone. These rooms were probably secret areas open only to the priesthood. Most of these temples' doorways show bar holes where doors or screens would have been fitted. The third and oldest of the temples, the East Temple, has a similar structure, although it must have been altered to accommodate the middle building. It has the remains of a small chamber built into the walls with a tiny hole from which perhaps an oracle spoke. Outside are the stone balls used to roll the huge slabs of stone into place, while behind the temple complex are the ruins of an even earlier building. To the right of the entrance gate is a stone block with cone-shaped indentations. The small stone balls found nearby suggest some kind of divination machine which predicted the future according to the movement of the balls. The National Museum of Archaeology in Valletta (➤ 93) has an artist's impression of what the temples once looked like.

✚ K4 ✉ Neolithic Temples Street, Tarxien ☎ 21695578 🕐 Daily 9–5 💷 Inexpensive 🍴 Nearest place in main square in Paola (€) 🚌 8, 11, 12, 13, 27, 29, 30, 133, 427 from Valletta; 800 from Gudja

Best
things
to do

Good places to have lunch

Amici Miei (€€)

This atmospheric eatery mixes a historic vaulted interior with contemporary design touches. The menu is casual, mixing pizzas with Mediterranean staples and a great outside terrace so you can take in the vista of the Grand Harbour and watch the world go by.
✉ Valletta Waterfront ☎ 21225000 🕐 Tue–Fri and Sun 11–3, 7–11, Sat 11–3, 6–midnight

L'Ankra (€€)

Walkable from the ferry at Mġarr harbour; good pizzas and some tasty local items.
✉ 11 Shore Street, Mġarr, Gozo ☎ 21555656 🕐 Daily 11:30–2:30, 6:30–10:30

Bloomers (€€)

Easy to find on the main road, next to Melita Pharmacy, with good Mediterranean-style food. Daily specials.
✉ St George's Road, St Julian's ☎ 21333394 🕐 Daily 12–2:30, 6:30–11:30

The Carriage (€€)

Great views across to Sliema and quality food. Superb home-made ravioli (ask, it's not on the menu), salads and French-style dishes.
✉ Valletta Buildings, South Street, Valletta ☎ 21247828 🕐 Mon–Fri 12–3, Fri–Sat 7:30–1

Crianza (€)

Pasta, pizza (take-away available), pancakes and salads in an ancient building. Often full but worth squeezing around a table.
✉ 33 Archbishop Street, Valletta ☎ 21238120 🕐 Daily 12–3:30, 6:30–11:30

Gillieru Restaurant (€€)

Reserve an outside table for a leisurely lunch overlooking the bay.
✉ 66 Church Street, St Paul's Bay ☎ 21573480 🕐 Daily 12:15–2:30

Ir-Rizzu (€€)

Seafood restaurant easily found on the seafront in Marsaxlokk.
The family has been catching or cooking fish for over 80 years.

✉ Xatt is-Sajjieda, Marsaxlokk ☎ 21871589

It-Tmun (€€)

Close to the Xlendi seafront in Gozo, this relaxing restaurant is
ideal for a slow lunch. Outside tables offer shade. The food is
Mediterranean, plus some Maltese dishes.

✉ 3 Mount Carmel Street, Xlendi, Gozo ☎ 21551571 🕐 Wed–Mon 12–3,
6–10:30 (closed Tue–Thu in Jan, most of Dec and Feb)

Pegasus (€€–€€€))

The best value at this brasserie-style restaurant is the set lunch.
A cool place for lunch with an ultra-contemporary decor.

✉ Le Meridien Phoenicia, The Mall, Floriana ☎ 22910162
🕐 Daily noon–11pm

Porto del Sol (€€)

Splendid views across Xemxija Bay and carefully cooked fish,
pasta and meat dishes in a comfortable and formal restaurant.
Good food and wine.

✉ Xemxija Road, St Paul's Bay ☎ 21573970 🕐 Mon–Sat 12–2:30, 6–11,
Sun 12–2:30

Best cathedrals and churches

Church of St Gregory, Żejtun (➤ 112–113)
– originally built by the Knights of St John, which held secrets revealed in the 1960s.

Church of St Lawrence, Vittoriosa (➤ 126)
– containing Mattia Preti's *tour de force*, the martyrdom of St Lawrence.

Church of St Nicholas, Siġġiewi (➤ 109)
– an exceptional example of the baroque style.

Church of St Philip, Żebbuġ (➤ 110)
– designed by local architect Tommaso Dingli.

Ħal-Millieri Church of the Annunciation, Żurrieq (➤ 113)
– decorated with 15th-century frescoes.

Mosta Rotunda, Mosta (➤ 138)
– whose dome is the fourth largest in Europe.

St George's Church, Victoria, Gozo (➤ 172)
– with a splendid gilded interior.

St John's Co-Cathedral, Valletta (➤ 48–49)
– ornate chapels dedicated to the Knights house a wealth of art treasures.

St Paul's Cathedral, Mdina (➤ 52–53)
– architect Lorenzo Gafà's baroque masterpiece.

St Paul's Church, Mdina (➤ 122–123)
– graced by a fine altarpiece by Preti; St Paul is said to have sheltered in the grotto below.

Top activities

A day by the water in Xlendi, Gozo (▶ 182): paddling, eating, drinking. It may be only a small beach but it is a great spot for swimming. Enjoying fresh seafood by the water is magical.

Fishing off a boat in Marsaxlokk (▶ 107) or St Paul's Bay (▶ 160–161). Get a taste of the sea from a charter boat

Jumping off the rocks into the deep blue sea. Try St Peter's Pool, a calm, natural pool halfway along the Delimara peninsula in the south of the island. Gets busy at weekends.

Learning to waterski or dive with options on both islands. There is some of the best diving in the Mediterranean, especially off the north coast of Malta and off Gozo's northwest corner. Sightings range from marine life to wartime wrecks. Many of the larger hotels arrange waterskiing.

Renting a bicycle and exploring the country roads of Gozo is a great way to see the island and it won't take too long to get round either (➤ 76).

Renting a car for a day to explore the west and southwest corner of Malta. Check out the Dingli Cliffs (➤ 104–105) for one of the best views on the island but make sure you leave the car and go for a stroll to really appreciate it.

Swimming in the Blue Lagoon on Comino Island (➤ 183) early in the morning. You need to be there early to avoid the armada of excursion boats that flock here. If you stay overnight you'll be first in the sea.

Taking a cruise around the Grand Harbour and admiring the sheer size of it (➤ 38–39). It is the biggest harbour in the Mediterranean and this is the best way to absorb it.

Walking in Gozo, especially in the Ta'Ċenċ area (➤ 177). Another good idea is to do a circular walk from Victoria, heading to Għasri, up to the sea, along the coast and stopping for lunch at Marsalforn, then back to Victoria. It's 11km (7 miles) long so you could always cycle or drive it.

Walking the Victoria Lines (➤ 143). This natural fault running across Malta was named after Queen Victoria and offers some great views across to Gozo.

Best beaches

Armier Beach. Situated in the extreme northeast of Malta (bus No 50 from Valletta), with occasional rough swells but lots of sand. This beach does get very busy in high season, when a couple of bars provide refreshments, but in low season everything is closed and it is almost deserted. Some water sports available.

Comino's beaches. The Blue Lagoon (➤ 183) is deservedly the most popular spot. Beautiful turquoise water and three tiny sandy beaches make this a busy destination.

Għajn Tuffieħa Bay. Pronounced 'ein tuff-ear', the name means 'eye (underground spring) of the apple'. You'll find it less crowded than Golden Bay beach – in fact Malta's least crowded sandy beach – yet only a short walk away and reached by steps (➤ 156–157).

Golden Bay. The most popular beach on the island after Mellieħa Bay because of its extensive stretch of sand (➤ 156–157). The shallow water makes it good for families but watch for warning flags if conditions get rough. Good water sports.

Ġnejna Bay. Without your own transport there is a 2km (1.2-mile) walk from Malta's Mġarr (➤ 158–159), but the worthwhile reward is sand with rocky platforms. Fishermen's huts and local families give this beach a more down-to-earth feel.

Marsaskala and St Thomas Bay. There is no sand but coastal bathing is very popular here because of the bay's picturesque location (➤ 106–107).

Mellieħa Bay. Malta's most popular beach (➤ 158) is 2km (1.2 miles) north of Mellieħa. Shallow water and lots of sand make it entirely suitable for children. Lots of water sports so not the place for serious swimmers.

Peter's Pool. Not much of a beach but a terrific jumping-off point into crystal-clear, deep water. Large flat rocks make good sunbathing perches and when it gets too hot just slip into the water to cool down.

Ramla Bay. Good-sized sandy beach in Gozo, shallow and safe for swimming except in rough conditions as there are reefs and dangerous currents. Loads of reddish-golden sand and a couple of snack bars. A lovely spot out of season is Gozo's San Blas beach.

Sliema/St Julian's. No sand but there are plenty of rocky platforms for sunbathing (➤ 140 and 142). Balluta Bay (➤ 140) between the two towns is a pretty spot with a small square of sand and rocks.

Drinks and snacks

DRINKS
Bajtra The word is Maltese for prickly pear, from which this very sweet liqueur is made. Drink when chilled.

Fernet Branca A 'digestive drink' (there's also one called averna) taken after eating a big meal. Swallow whole; tastes foul.

Cisk Every Mediterranean island has its lager and Malta is no exception. Cisk (pronounced *chisk*) is quite a weak affair, Cisk Export is the stronger and tastier option. As an alternative, the hangovers from British rule are Hop Leaf Pale Ale and Farson's Bitter Shandy.

Kinnie Malta's very own herbal soft drink and local answer to Coca-Cola but with a more adult taste and often taken as an aperitif. For an alcoholic version try a tamakari kinnie cocktail – one of the island's most popular liqueurs, diluted with kinnie – ideally before an evening meal.

Maltese wine Malta has finally got on the map with its wines Marsovin and Delicata. The latter is being praised by foreign wine critics. They may cost a bit more but they are worth it. Gozo is well known for its strong, full-bodied red wines.

FOOD
Bigilla Bread with crushed garlic, and broad beans served as a dip. Sold in packets from street carts, it is a Maltese speciality and something of an acquired taste.

Figolli Iced biscuits with almond and lemon, usually only available at Easter time.

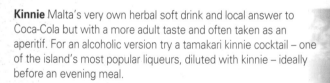

Gozo cheese Known as *gbejna*. The peppered version is the best, though some eat the unpeppered cheese for breakfast.

Maltese bread Absolutely delicious if eaten freshly baked. If you are up early enough purchase it from the mobile breadman. The rustic *hobz biz-zejt* is a roll rubbed with tomatoes which is then drizzled with olive oil, filled with tuna and salad and served with olives and capers.

Pastizzi Small savoury puff pastries filled with local ricotta cheese and/or spinach or peas. This is a common mid-morning or early evening snack.

Best views and natural sights

Water sports

Diving
Scuba divers are well catered for and 30–40m (100–130ft) dives can be enjoyed with clear visibility. The tourist board has a map showing the most popular dive sites and other helpful information. **The Professional Diving Schools Association** has details of all registered diving companies.

✉ PO Box 12, St Paul's Bay ☎ www.pdsa.org.mt

Jetskiing
As in most popular beach holiday destinations, jetskiis are readily available. Always rent from a reputable establishment – check with the tourist office – and take all the necessary safety precautions.

Paragliders and inflatables
Many resorts provide excitement either in the air or on the sea. For a more sedate trip around the bay take a canoe or pedalo.

Sailing and yachting
Between Malta, Gozo and Comino there are nearly 30 anchorages, and places to rent boats include Marsamxett Harbour and Mellieħa Bay. The Royal Malta Yacht Club at Manoel Island (tel: 21333109; www.rmyc.org) has information on the chartering of yachts. Enquire also at the Viking Sailing Club Nautical School, Floriana (tel: 21236911) or Malta Yacht Charters (10 St Lawrence Street, Sliema; tel: 21388254; www.maltayachtcharters.com).

Adira Sailing School
✉ Għadira Bay ☎ 21523190; www.adirasailingcentre.com.mt

Nautica
✉ 21/23 Msida Road, Gżira ☎ 21345138; www.nautica.com.mt

Snorkelling
Check out the local marine life with a snorkel, mask and flippers. Both snorkellers and divers should fly a code-A flag or tow a surface marker buoy to alert speedboat traffic. Popular spots

include the coast just north of Baħar-iċ-Ċagħaq, while a more deserted place is the Għar Qawqla beach near Hotel Calypso at Marsalforn, Gozo.

Sportfishing
Fishing Mania has a boat insured for up to six people with a qualified captain. It leaves Marsaskala or Ta'Xbiex at 8:30am and returns in the afternoon. There is also an 8:30pm departure for night bottom fishing, returning at 2am. Rates include tackle, bait and snacks.
✉ Fishing Mania, 20, Flat 4, Old Anchor Court, Buttar Street, Marsaskala
☎ 99822012 (mobile); www.mol.net.mt/Fishingmania 🚌 19, 20, 21

Swimming
It's cheap, it's fun and there are plenty of opportunities around the islands. Check the choice of beaches (➤ 64–65) that provide the best swimming for you and your family.

Waterskiing
Waterskiing can be arranged through the larger hotels at St Paul's Bay, Mellieħa Bay, Sliema, St George's Bay and Golden Bay.
✉ Paradise Diving and Watersports, Paradise Bay Hotel, Ċirkewwa
☎ 21524363; www.paradisediving.com

Windsurfing
Windsurfing may be enjoyed at a number of hotels fronting the sheltered northern bays. Alpha School of English (tel: 21581474; www.alphaschoolmalta.com) offers several water sports courses including beginners windsurfing and level two for more advanced sportspeople. Others include the Corinthia Hotel (tel: 21374114; www.corinthiahotels.com) at St George's Bay (➤ 146).

Places to take the children

Eden Super Bowl and Cinemas
Consisting of a computerized bowling alley with 20 lanes, a bar and a huge multi-cinema complex. The Paceville location means there are plenty of fast-food type restaurants close by.
✉ Paceville, St George's Bay ☎ 23710777 (reservations) ⏰ Daily 10am–12:30am 🚌 62, 64, 67, 68, 70 from Valletta; 627 between Paceville and Marsaxlokk

Fort Rinella
Volunteers in 19th-century costume conduct a tour of the fort and conclude with a bayonet practice display with non-obligatory audience participation.
✉ St Rocco Road, Kalkara ☎ 21809713; www.wirtartna.org ⏰ Daily 9:30–5. Activity tour daily 2:30 🚌 4 from Valletta and a 10-min walk

Mdina Dungeons
Pass through Mdina Gate and these medieval dungeon chambers are immediately on your right: 'Discover Horror, Drama and Mysteries from the Dark Past'.
✉ St Publius Square, Mdina ☎ 21450267 ⏰ Daily 9:30–4 🚌 80, 83, 86

Mediterranean Marine Park
Dolphins and sea lions, reptiles, swans, wallabies and other creatures are found cavorting here and putting on shows each day.
✉ White Rocks, Baħar iċ-Ċagħaq ☎ 21372218; www.mediterraneo.com.mt ⏰ Mar–Oct daily 10–5; Nov–early Jan and Feb Tue–Sun 10–1:30. Closed mid-Jan to mid-Feb 🚌 68 from Valletta; 70 from Buġibba; 70, 645 from Sliema

Multimedia events
Older children should enjoy some of the multimedia 'experiences'. The Wartime Experience (➤ 100) is best reserved for teenagers. And don't forget the historical parades at Fort St Elmo (➤ 90).

Splash & Fun Park

Splash & Fun Park has four water chutes, a large pool and a restaurant. Adjacent, the Children's Play Park is free to enter and features model dinosaurs, bouncy castles, bumper cars and the like.

✉ White Rocks, Baħar iċ-Ċagħaq

☎ 21374283; www.splashandfun.com.mt

⏱ Late Apr–end Jun and mid-Sep to early Nov daily 9–5:30; Jul–early Sep daily 9–9. Closed mid-Nov to late Apr

🚌 68 from Valletta; 70 from Sliema or Buġibba

Toy Museum

This is an enjoyable collection of toys for adults as well as children, with some exhibits dating back to the 1790s.

✉ 10 Gnien Xibla Street, Xagħra, Gozo

☎ 21562489 ⏱ Apr Thu–Sat 10–1; May to mid-Oct Mon–Sat 10–12, 3–6; Nov–Mar Sat and public hols 10–1

🚌 64, 65 from Victoria

Underwater Safari

Children should enjoy a trip in an observation keel; it's below the level of the sea with windows for viewing the marine life, including the odd passing octopus. For details (➤ 154).

a walk

around Valletta

This walk begins past the Triton Fountain and goes through the City Gate, once the main entrance into the citadel.

Take the first right into Ordnance Street, passing La Vittoria (▶ 91) and the post office next to it on the corner of Castille Square.

The imposing Auberge de Castille (▶ 83) is opposite, on the corner with Triq il-Merkanti (Merchants Street). Here is a bustling scene where bargains can be found and there is a morning market.

Walk down Merchants Street, and take the second left, signed for St John's Co-Cathedral (▶ 48–49) but return to Merchants Street for the next right turn into Triq Santa Lucia (St Lucia Street) and the Church of St Paul's Shipwreck (▶ 84–85). Return to the Merchants Street junction and cross straight over, then turn right into Republic Street and Republic Square (▶ 95).

It may be time for an alfresco drink or meal in the tree-lined square or a visit to the entertaining Great Siege of Malta and the Knights of St John Exhibition (➤ 91), which is tucked away by Café Premier, next to the Bibliotheca.

Continue the walk by turning left into Triq'it-Teatru (Old Theatre Street), on the corner of the square, crossing three junctions and passing the delightful Manoel Theatre (➤ 92–93) before turning right into West Street. Continue down this street until you reach the sea wall, where a right turn brings Fort St Elmo (➤ 90) into view.

Head for the fort alongside the massive city walls overlooking St Elmo Bay, taking time to contemplate the awesome defences. This walk ends at Fort St Elmo at the point.

Distance 2km (1.2 miles)
Time 2–4 hours, depending on visits
Start point City Gate ✚ *Valletta b5*
End point Fort St Elmo ✚ *Valletta g2*
🛈 Tourist Information, 1 City Arcades ☎ 21237747
Lunch Eddie's Café Regina (➤ 98)

Sport and leisure

ATHLETICS
The Malta Amateur Athletics Association
Cross-country and track-and-field events are held regularly.
✉ 7 Racecourse Street, Marsa ☎ 21423834; www.athleticsmalta.org

BOWLING
For a game of 10-pin bowling visit the Eden Super Bowl (➤ 72).

CYCLING
With everywhere in relatively close proximity, Gozo is one of the best places to take to two wheels. To rent a bike check out the following companies: **On Two Wheels** ✉ 36 Rabat Road, Marsalforn, Gozo ☎ 21561503; **Better Living** ✉ 39 Nazju Ellul Street, Gżira ☎ 21310756; **Magri Cycles and Spares** ✉ Mberraq Garage, Vetsru Street, Xagħra ☎ 21551468

GOLF
The 18-hole course at the Marsa Sports Club has had some 50 sand bunkers added. Temporary membership at the Marsa Sports Club (see opposite) allows visitors to use the course.
Royal Malta Golf Club
✉ Marsa Sports Club, Aldo Moro Street, Marsa ☎ 21227019; www.royalmaltagolfclub.com

HEALTH CLUBS
A number of the better hotels have health and leisure clubs with excellent facilities. The best of all is the Atheneum Spa at the Corinthia Palace Hotel and Spa, Balzan (➤ 146), but there are others such as the Kempinski San Lawrenz in Gozo (➤ 184).
☎ 22110000; www.kempinski-gozo.com

HORSE-BACK RIDING
For some of the most scenic rides try the Golden Bay Horse Riding School, which offers a one-hour trek along the coastal path

or two hours to Anchor Bay. You don't need to be experienced and children are welcome, but there is a weight limit for riders.
✉ Golden Bay ☎ 21573360

HORSE RACING
An abiding passion with islanders but not how most of us know it. Here jockeys are not astride their beast but sit behind in a very flimsy-looking trap, similar to a chariot, in which they are dragged along at breakneck pace. The horse-racing stadium (www.malta racingclub.com) is next door to the Marsa Sports Club (see below).

SPORTS CENTRES
Marsa Sports Club
The island's largest sports centre, 4km (2.5 miles) south of Valletta, with golf, cricket ground, mini golf, tennis courts, squash courts, billiards, fitness centre and swimming pool.
✉ Aldo Moro Street, Marsa ☎ 21233851 🕐 Mon–Fri 9–9, Sat–Sun 9–5; www.marsasportsclub.com

SOCCER
Soccer games are mostly played between September and May. The National Stadium at Ta' Qali is the best place to view a match.
Malta Football Association
✉ The National Football Stadium, Millennium Stand 2nd Floor, Ta' Qali
☎ 21411505; www.mfa.com.mt

Exploring

Despite the fact that Malta has some of the oldest sites in the Mediterranean, a remarkable and at times turbulent history, natural scenic beauty and secluded areas, it is known mainly for its package tours and beach holidays. Explore the island and its little sister, Gozo, and you will find so much more. Relive the history in the capital, Valletta, and the towns of Vittoriosa and Mdina. Find out more about the brave and remarkable Maltese people and seek out some of the quieter unspoilt places of natural beauty. Rent a car to visit other parts of the island away from your holiday accommodation to get a real feel of the place. Walking or cycling in Gozo is a pleasure and you can stumble on a traditional way of life, still in existence despite the onset of tourism. If it is water sports you want, you will find no shortage, and some of the best diving in the Mediterranean can be found off the shores of Gozo.

Valletta

All roads lead to Valletta. Nearly every bus route on the island starts and ends in the capital and anyone visiting Malta for the first time will spend some time here.

The city was built after the Great Siege to create an impregnable fortress against another assault. It retains the feel of a fortified city, but is much more than a defensive town. Valletta was built as a home for the aristocratic Order of the Knights of St John, which ensured exemplary architecture, in a culturally rich Renaissance city. Despite intensive bombing during World War II, the city remains a coherent whole and is visually imposing. The streets were built on a simple grid-plan but rocky terrain meant few level surfaces. The constantly shifting levels bring to mind Byron's 'cursed streets of stairs' (*Farewell to Malta*, 1811).

VALLETTA

Francesco Laparelli da Cortona, a military engineer, arrived in Malta in 1565. His brief was to help plan a city that would permanently minimize the Turkish threat. A rocky peninsula in the north of the island was chosen as the site for a completely new city and what you see today is largely unchanged from what Laparelli planned and what his Maltese assistant, Geralamo

Cassar, filled with extraordinary architecture. Valletta was the first planned city in Europe.

Everyone enters Valletta through the City Gate and passes directly into the pedestrianized Republic Street. It is the spine of the city that runs in a straight line for 1.5km (1 mile) to Fort St Elmo (► 90), at the northeast tip of the peninsula. The street passes across a number of squares, each rich in history and architecture, with bisecting side streets that lead down to one of the two enclosing harbours. Driving into Valletta is pointless because of its small size and 'streets of stairs', but this makes it ideal for walking. The city changes character during the course of the day, the best time to visit being the morning, when shops, restaurants, churches and museums are open and there is a buzz to this tiny metropolis. The afternoons are suitable for leisurely walks, but the streets are then devoid of people and most places are closed for an enviably long siesta. Early evening is a little more animated, especially at weekends, but the nights are strangely quiet as Valletta retreats into itself.

✚ K3

ℹ️ City Gate ☎ 21237747

Auberge de Castille

The Auberge de Castille is strategically located close to the ramparts and it is the city's most impressive example of *auberge* architecture. It dates from 1574 but the imposing baroque facade was added in the mid-18th century under Grandmaster Pinto, a flamboyant bust of whom decorates the top of the stately doorway. Another admirable feature is the cornice that frames the building's roof and blends harmoniously with the louvred windows. The overall effect is that of baroque architecture at its most graceful and least complicated. The British Army had its headquarters here, and today it houses the prime minister's office.

✚ *Valletta d5* ✉ Castille Square 🚫 Not open to the public 🍴 Cafés and restaurants (€–€€) in walking distance

Bibliotheca (National Library)

This grand, late 18th-century, Venetian-style building was the last public building commissioned by the Knights. It now houses some 400,000 works, many rare or priceless, and a small selection is on display in the main hall, including the 12th-century Papal Bull instituting the Order of Knights and the 1530 Deed of Donation of Malta to the Order by Charles V. The walls of the hall are lined with books in their fine bindings. All archival material covering the history of the Knights from 1113 to 1798 is lodged in the library and it is an important source of research material for historians.

✚ *Valletta d4* ✉ Republic Square ☎ 21236585 🕓 Oct to mid-Jun Mon–Fri 8:30–5:45, Sat 8:15–1; late Jun–Sep Mon–Fri 8:30–1:15, Sat 8:15–1 ✋ Free
🍴 Cafés (€–€€) in Republic Square

Casa Rocca Piccola

This late 16th-century dwelling is the ancestral home of the de Piro family of the Knights of St John and is worth visiting for its period antiques. The bedroom contains a beautiful four-poster bed, the library has an intriguing wall-cabinet that functioned as a portable chapel and the various other rooms have a fascinating variety of antiques and paintings.

✚ *Valletta e3* ✉ 74 Republic Street ☎ 21221499 🕓 Mon–Sat 10–4. Guided tours on the hour (last tour 4pm) ✋ Expensive 🍴 Cafés and restaurants (€–€€) within walking distance

Church of St Paul's Shipwreck

Originally designed by Gerolamo Cassar in the 16th century, the Church of St Paul's Shipwreck underwent extensive modifications and gained a number of adornments that are now its chief attractions. These include ceiling frescoes, an altarpiece by the Florentine artist Paladini, and a piece of St Paul's wristbone behind a glass case on an altar. Another altar contains part of the block on which St Paul is said to have been beheaded in Rome, to be seen indistinctly from a distance. The statue of St Paul, by Melchiorre Gaffa, is carried through the streets on 10 February, the day St Paul's shipwreck (➤ 160–161) is commemorated.

✝ *Valletta e4* ✉ Triq San Pawl (St Paul's Street) ☎ 21223348 🕐 Daily 9–7, except during Mass ✋ Free 🍴 Cafés and restaurants (€) within walking distance

Floriana

This pleasant suburb of Valletta is best explored on foot (► 88–89), and although largely rebuilt after World War II, there are some notable reminders of the past. Paolo Floriani was an Italian military engineer sent by the Pope in 1634 to further strengthen Valletta with a secondary defence system (Floriana Lines) outside the city.

The largest structure is **St Publius Church,** which was finally completed in 1792, nearly 40 years after the first stone was laid, while its classical portico is a late 19th-century addition. The entire edifice was largely rebuilt after extensive damage during World War II. The vast open space in front of the church is distinguished by a number of large stone caps, which are the protruding lids to over 70 granary pits. The pits were dug in the 17th century to store food safely and they were used again from 1941 to 1943 when Malta was once more under siege.

One of the most singular churches in Malta is the circular and compact **Sarria Church,** built in 1676 to fulfil a vow that was made by the Order of St John at the height of a terrible plague earlier in the year. Opposite the church is the Wignacourt Water Tower, an elaborate fountain that was constructed under Grand-master Wignacourt in 1615, part of an aqueduct system built to supply Valletta with water from the hills around Mdina. The nearby

Argotti Botanical Gardens, with exotic trees and rare cacti, offer an escape from the traffic that pours through Floriana. So too does Maglio Gardens, a cultured strip of garden that stretches from the Argotti gardens back towards Valletta.

✚ *Valletta a6* ✉ Immediate south of Valletta, a short walk from the bus terminal ⏰ St Publius Church open for services Sat evening and Sun morning. Sarria Church Sun service at 10:30am ⑪ Restaurants (€–€€) within walking distance

a walk in Floriana

To see Floriana and have an interesting, pleasing stroll, begin at the Phoenicia Hotel, on Il-Mall.

With your back to the Phoenicia Hotel's entrance, turn right and walk down to the Independence Monument in the middle of the road. The entrance to the Maglio Gardens is immediately behind the statue. Enter the park, designed by a Grandmaster as a place for young knights to exercise by playing a ball game in a large, narrow structure, since

demolished. The shaded pathway is dotted with busts of various Maltese dignitaries. Over to the left the notable flat caps of the subterranean granary silos can clearly be seen in the huge square in front of St Publius Church (▶ 86).

At the end of the park's walkway exit on the left side to view the Wignacourt Water Tower and Sarria Church (▶ 86) on the other side of the road. Enter Argotti Botanical Gardens (▶ 86) by the side of the water tower. The gardens, dating from the late 18th century, are well maintained and there are a number of cacti and exotic trees to see. At the end of the walkway there is a good view from the balcony of the suburbs stretching across to Marsamxett Harbour.

Retrace your steps to the park's entrance and cross the road to the Sarria Church. Follow the road down to the right until it meets the main road at a junction with a statue of a decrepit-looking lion gracing a fountain. Turn left and walk up the main road towards Valletta, past shops and the American Consular office, to a roundabout. Keep to the left and the Phoenicia Hotel will be seen again on the other side of the car park.

Distance 2km (1.2 miles)
Time 1 hour
Start/end point Phoenicia Hotel ✚ *Valletta a5*
Lunch Phoenicia Hotel (€€€) ✉ Il-Mall
☎ 21225241

Fort St Elmo

The vulnerable tip of the Valletta peninsula was chosen by the Order of St John as the best site for their fortifications, and the fort they built was sorely tested 13 years later in 1565 when the Turks laid siege. The fort withstood the attack for 31 days. The Knights were eventually forced to surrender, but the Turks' pyrrhic victory – their losses were more than four times those of the Christians – only served to endorse the value of St Elmo, and so the fort was rebuilt and enlarged. Its star-shaped design allowed for watchtowers to be strategically angled so as to guard the entrances to both harbours and the British added gun emplacements in the 19th and 20th centuries. The fort, used in the making of the film *Midnight Express* (1978), where the interior scenes stood in for those of an Istanbul prison, is currently closed to the public except during **Alarme! Battle re-enactments**.

✚ *Valletta g2* ✉ End of Republic Street and Merchants Street ☎ 21222430

Alarme! Battle re-enactments

☎ 22915136 (tickets) 🕐 Battle re-enactments at 11am on Sun in mid-Oct and mid-Nov (check exact date with the tourist office) ✋ Moderate

Great Siege of Malta and the Knights of St John Exhibition

An entertaining and fun way to learn about the Knights of St John. This attraction offers a concise trip through some of the crucial historical turning points for the Knights as they leave the Holy Land and settle on Malta, and the subsequent battles with the Ottoman forces that resulted in the Great Siege of 1566. It's a walk-through exhibition that takes around 45 minutes, but innovative use of technology, surround sound and 3-D dioramas keeps everyone entertained. You become part of the plot as you take on the passive role of Christian pilgrim visiting the Holy Land. Collect your portable CD player (13 different languages available) and you can enjoy the exhibitions at your own pace. The graphics

are impressive and children should love it. **www.**greatsiege.com.mt

✚ *Valletta d4* ✉ Republic Square ☎ 21247300
🕐 Daily 10–4 ✋ Moderate 🍴 Cafés (€–€€) in Square

La Vittoria (Church of Our Lady of Victories)

This church's appearance belies its historical significance, being Valletta's first place of worship when it was built in 1567 to commemorate the end of the siege, and now the oldest building in Valletta. La Vittoria was the main place of worship for the Knights of St John for a decade after the siege as the island recovered from the Ottoman onslaught, and Grandmaster Jean Parisot de la Vallette (after whom the new city of Valletta was named) was originally buried here after his death in 1568. However, when the Church (now Co-Cathedral) of St John was completed in 1577, la Vallette's remains were transferred to this more impressive place of worship.

✚ *Valletta c5* ✉ Ordnance Street 🍴 Cafés and restaurants (€) within walking distance

Manoel Theatre

Commissioned by the Knights of the Order of St John, this theatre opened in 1732. After a long period of disuse, then conversion to a hostel for the homeless and later a cinema, this gem of a theatre was beautifully restored in 1960. The stalls area is tiny, as is the

stage, but enclosing both are three tiers of ornately decorated boxes in soft green and gold and above them a gallery area from where a spectator could reach out and touch the gilded ceiling, which has a solitary chandelier in its centre. If there is an opportunity to see any performance do not hesitate to book; the theatre season runs from October to May. The courtyard café is always worth a visit in its own right to relax over a drink or have a light meal.

✚ *Valletta d3* ✉ Triq it-Teatru il-Qadim (Old Theatre Street) ☎ 21222618 (theatre), 21242977 (museum); www.teatrumanoel.com.mt 🕓 Guided tours: Mon–Fri 10:15, 11, 11:45, 12:30, 1:15, 2, 2:45, 3:30; Sat 10:15, 11, 11:45, 12:30 ✋ Moderate

National Museum of Archaeology

The National Museum of Archaeology building was once the Auberge de Provence, built in 1575 and home to the most prestigious group of Knights. Although it has undergone some considerable modification over the centuries, it still has its main hall where the Knights would dine on iced dishes (remarkably, the ice came from Sicily). The building now houses an important collection of antiquities, and a visit is recommended as a preliminary to seeing the major prehistoric sites in Malta and Gozo. There are important sculptures from the Tarxien Temples (➤ 54–55), including the bulbous lower half of a fertility goddess that would have stood over 2m (6ft) high. From Ħaġar Qim (➤ 40–41) there is a superb limestone altar and a number of Roman antiquities, including a huge anchor that was discovered off the northern coast in the 1960s.

✚ *Valletta c4* ✉ Republic Street ☎ 21221623 🕓 Daily 9–7 ✋ Inexpensive 🍴 Cafés and restaurants (€) within walking distance

National Museum of Fine Arts

Best places to see, ➤ 44–45.

National War Museum

Located under the ramparts facing Marsamxett
Harbour, the vaulted hall of the War Museum is
packed with hardware, photographs and memorabilia from World
War II, and gives a good account of conditions in Malta between
1939 and 1945. One of the most famous exhibits is the wingless
Gladiator biplane, *Faith*, the sole survivor of the *Faith, Hope* and
Charity trio of planes that formed Malta's aerial defence in 1940.
Also on display is the George Cross that the people of Malta
received for their heroism in 1942.

✚ *Valletta g2* ✉ Lower St Elmo on French Curtain ☎ 21222430 ⏰ Daily
9–5 👋 Inexpensive 🍴 Nearest café (€) is at the Sacra Infermeria

Palace of the Grandmasters

Best places to see, ➤ 46–47.

Republic Square (Misraħ Ir-Repubblika)

The surrounding cafés and their outdoor tables have made this centrally located square a natural meeting place. It was called Queen's Square under the British, who reinforced the point by placing a statue of Queen Victoria here in 1891. The lace-clad queen now surveys the tourists, who enjoy watching the world go by under the superb backdrop of the Bibliotheca (➤ 84).

✚ *Valletta d3* ✉ Republic Square 🍴 Eddie's Café Regina (➤ 98)

Sacra Infermeria

The Order of St John may have degenerated into an aristocrats' club but it began life as an association of noble hospitallers, so not surprisingly the Holy Infirmary (Sacra Infermeria) was one of Valletta's earliest buildings, receiving its first patients in 1574. In the mid-17th century Grandmaster Nicholas Cotoner was responsible for the inauguration of a School of Anatomy and Surgery. It was then considered one of the most important hospitals in Europe and could accommodate almost a thousand patients. It remained in active use as a hospital until 1918 under French and then British military control. During World War II it was seriously bomb-damaged and after extensive renovation, reopened as the Mediterranean Conference Centre. See the excellent Malta Experience (➤ 100) audio-visual film show here in a modern auditorium and experience **The Knights Hospitallers,** a well planned walk-through attraction with high-tech dioramas depicting scenes from pivotal moments in the history of the Knights Hospitallers.

✚ *Valletta g3* ✉ Mediterranean Street ☎ 21243840 🕐 Mon–Fri 9:30–4:30, Sat–Sun 9:30–4 👋 Inexpensive 🍴 Café (€) ❓ Conducted tours

The Knights Hospitallers
✉ Mediterranean Conference Centre/Sacra Infermeria ☎ 21224135
🕐 Daily 9:30–4:30 (last admission 3:30) ✋ Inexpensive

St John's Co-Cathedral and Museum
Best places to see, ➤ 48–49.

Upper Barrakka Gardens
These 18th-century gardens on top of St Peter and St Paul's demi-bastion were planned as a roofed playground for Italian knights but the arches are the only reminder that the place was once covered. Now open to the air, the gardens offer views of the Grand Harbour (➤ 38–39) and Vittoriosa across the water and also provide one of the best places for a picnic in Valletta. The gardens are dotted with statues, the most interesting being Sciortino's *Les Gavroches*.

🔀 *Valletta d5* ✉ Castille Place
🍴 Cafés and restaurants (€)

Valletta Waterfront
Valletta's waterfront has been redeveloped since 2005 and the historic baroque warehouses built by Grandmaster Pinto, plus the Forni Stores erected by the Knights in 1626, have been renovated and now form part of a leisure complex comprising shops, bars and restaurants. Malta's cruise port is here, which means that vast leviathans of the sea are docked at the terminal, dwarfing the surrounding buildings.

🔀 *Valletta c6 (off map)*

HOTELS

Grand Harbour Hotel (€)

A superb location with outstanding views of the Grand Harbour (➤ 38–39) and an inexpensive restaurant. Rooms can be small and facilities are basic but nevertheless this still represents value for money.

✉ 47 Battery Street, Valletta ☎ 21246003; www.grandharbourhotel.com

Grand Hotel Excelsior (€€€)

Set just outside the walls of Valletta, this luxury option offers an excellent range of facilities, including a spa and fitness centre, and a diving and water-sports centre. There are also three restaurants on site.

✉ Great Siege Road, Floriana ☎ 21250520; www.excelsior.com.mt

Hotel Osborne (€€)

The Osborne is a smart place to have a room if staying in Valletta. It has an air of elegance, a pleasant dining room, a bar and a lounge area. Popular with British and German visitors.

✉ 50 South Street, Valletta ☎ 21232127; www.osbornehotel.com

RESTAURANTS

Amici Miei (€€)

See page 58.

Blue Room (€€–€€€)

Just by the palace, this is one of the best Chinese restaurants in Malta. The menu has a number of set meals, and house specials include beef in black pepper and bean curd with minced pork.

✉ 59 Republic Street, Valletta ☎ 21238014 🕔 Tue–Sat 12–3, 7–11

Café Jubilee (€)

This is a popular bistro decked out in 1920/30s style. The daily specials are recommended, though there is a menu of standard pasta and salad dishes.

✉ 125 St Lucy Street, Valletta ☎ 21252332 🕔 Daily 8am–1am

Café Premier (€)

Outdoor tables in Republic Square, ideal for people-watching, and a musty interior that looks unchanged from decades ago. Set meals, pizzas, pasta, burgers and a fairly good vegetarian salad.

✉ Republic Square, Valletta ☎ 21234385 🕐 Daily 8:30–5:30

Cocopazzo (€)

A neat little restaurant, suitable for lunch or dinner, away from the noise of Republic Street. Salads, pasta, chicken and fish dishes.

✉ Valletta Buildings, South Street ☎ 21235706 🕐 Mon–Fri 9–3, 6:30–10, Sat–Sun 12–3, 6:30–10

Eddie's Café Regina (€)

Pizzas, pastas, grills, milkshakes and one or two Maltese dishes, including *qarabali* (stuffed marrows).

✉ Republic Square, Valletta ☎ 21246454 🕐 Daily 10–10

Da Pippo (€€)

Da Pippo has also been discovered by discerning Maltese judging from the stream of locals popping in for lunch. The menu of Italian and Maltese dishes should satisfy most tastes.

✉ 136 Melita Street ☎ 21248029 🕐 Mon–Sat 11:30–3:30

Scalini (€€)

This upmarket restaurant is set in a vaulted building. The refined decor is matched by the equally refined menu featuring continental meat dishes and fresh seafood.

✉ 320 South Street (opposite the Museum of Fine Arts), Valletta ☎ 21244531; www.scalini-restaurant.com 🕐 Mon–Sat 6–11

Trabuxu (€)

Malta's first wine bar that sells good value meals and tapas in addition to locally produced wines. The clientele is mainly local, including many politicians and civil servents from surrounding offices and city enterprises.

✉ 1 id-Dejqa Street ☎ 21223036 🕐 Daily noon–11pm

SHOPPING

ARTS, CRAFTS AND ANTIQUES

Artisans Centre
Close to the tourist information office is one of the best shops for quality handicrafts. There are handsome Maltese crosses on chains, picture frames, prints, souvenirs and gifts.

✉ 9 and 10 Freedom Square ☎ 21246216 🕐 Mon–Fri 9–1, 4–7, Sat 9–1

Bristow Pottery
Sells a selection of hand-thrown Maltese pottery.

✉ Valletta Waterfront ☎ 21226782 🕐 Daily 10–8

Galea Paintings
The studio and gallery of the artist Aldo Galea. The subject is Malta, especially shipping scenes. Posting and packing service.

✉ 8 Triq il-Merkanti (Merchants Street), Valletta ☎ 21243591 🕐 Mon–Fri 9:30–1, 4–7, Sat 9:15–12:45

Gio. Batta Delia
Fine chinaware and glass from around the world – Wedgwood, Waterford, Spode, Belleek, Minton, Dresden, Cristal Lalique – and an export service.

✉ Ferreria Palace, 307 Republic Street, Valletta ☎ 21233618

MARKETS

Indoor Market
Valletta's indoor market is devoted mostly to food and this is the place to visit the day before you leave Malta to make a last-minute purchase of *gbejna* (Gozitan cheese).

✉ Triq il-Merkanti (Merchants Street) where the open-air market ends
🕐 Mon–Sat 6:30am–1pm

Open-air markets
There are two open-air markets in Valletta. Merchants Street is mostly clothes, accessories, religious icons, CDs and videos. On Sunday a very busy market opens up in St James' Ditch, near the Triton Fountain, with a more interesting collection of bric-a-brac.

✉ Triq il-Merkanti (Merchants Street) and St James' Ditch, Valletta ⏱ Triq il-Merkanti: Mon–Sat 7–noon; St James' Ditch: Sun 6:30am–1pm

SOUVENIRS
The Silversmith's Shop
A good place to see a range of sterling silver objects, including some lovely traditional filigree.
✉ Triq Borg Maurice ☎ 21231495 ⏱ Mon–Fri 10–12:30, 4:30–9, Sat 10–12:30

ENTERTAINMENT

The Malta Experience
The theatre is set inside the historic 16th-century Sacra Infermeria (➤ 95) and the show sets itself the daunting task of presenting Malta's history from neolithic times onwards in 50 minutes. With the help of 3,000 colour slides and 39 projectors it does this well.
✉ St Elmo Bastion, Mediterranean Street, Valetta ☎ 21243776; www.themaltaexperience.com ⏱ Mon–Fri on the hour 11–4, Sat–Sun 11am–1pm. Oct–Jun extra performance at 2pm

St James Cavalier Centre for Creativity
Films, theatre, music recitals and art exhibitions take place here.
✉ Ordnance Street ☎ 21223200; www.sjcav.org ⏱ Mon–Sat 10–10, Sun 10–5

The Wartime Experience
A film covering Malta during the years of World War II and made up of archive film recording what happened and the suffering endured by the Maltese people. Highly recommended.
✉ Embassy Complex, St Lucia's Street, Valletta ☎ 21227436 ⏱ Daily 10–1; on the hour, every hour

BAR
The Pub
Also known as Ollie's Last Stand, as this was the pub where actor Oliver Reed collapsed and died during the filming of *Gladiator*.
✉ 136 Archbishop Street, Valletta ☎ 79807042 (mobile) ⏱ Daily 10–4

Marsaxlokk

The South

A growing number of visitors are discovering the charms of Malta's south, hitherto left off the tourist trail. Sadly, the lack of tourism here does not guarantee unspoiled landscapes, as the south is the site of Luqa airport and the old Ħal Far military base (now an unsightly industrial estate) and industry and quarries have left their mark on the land.

But there is also much here that is worth exploring. Marsaxlokk is still a picturesque fishing village, unsung Dingli Cliffs offer spectacular views, and the Blue Grotto boasts sparkling sapphire seas. Ħal Saflieni Hypogeum is a world-class archaeological site, and the fascinating temples such as Ħaġar Qim, Mnajdra and Tarxien provide an insight into the island's ancient past.

BIRŻEBBUĠA

Despite the seaside setting, Birżebbuġa is not recommended as a resort – the water is sometimes polluted – but its prehistoric cliff cave of Għar Dalam and museum are well worth seeing. The cave was first inhabited by Stone Age humans around 4000BC (the last occupants were evicted in 1911) but excavations have revealed animal bones that go back some quarter of a million years: dwarf elephants, bears and hippopotamuses. More remains of animals have been found that may have lived within a cave only 145m (475ft) long; the cave somehow functioned as a natural trap for animals.

✚ K6 ✉ 10km (6 miles) southeast of Valletta. Għar

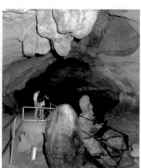

Dalam is 1km (0.5 miles) north of Birżebbuġa 🕐 Daily 9–5 👋 Moderate 🍴 Restaurant (€–€€) at the Seabreeze Hotel in Pretty Bay (▶ 114) 🚌 11–13, 15, 110, 113

BLUE GROTTO

The Blue Grotto experience is a half-hour trip along the coast by colourfully painted boat from Wied-iż-Żurrieq, passing through a series of natural sea caves with picturesque rock formations. Its popularity with tour coaches can mean waiting in a queue, so try to arrive early in the morning.

✚ H6 ✉ Wied-iż-Żurrieq, 3km
(2 miles) southwest of Żurrieq
☎ 21640058 🕐 Daily 8–4
✋ Expensive 🍴 Cafés (€)
between the car park and the
sea 🚌 38, 138

BUSKETT GARDENS

These charming woodland
gardens were created for
Grandmaster Lascaris in the
17th century with the practical
purpose of raising hunting
falcons. Today they offer
welcoming shade during the
heat of the summer.

The name is taken from
boschetto ('little wood') and
the gardens reveal a
botanically diverse collection
of trees, including pine, oak
and cypress, as well as groves
of oranges and olives. It is the
perfect place to picnic and
many Maltese families do just
that at weekends. It is the only
woodland area on the island
and is particularly delightful
in spring.

✚ F4 ✉ 4km (2.5 miles) south
of Rabat ✋ Free 🍴 Light
refreshments available, but a
picnic is recommended 🚌 81

CLAPHAM JUNCTION

This network of cart ruts, parallel grooves cut into the rock that sometimes cross each other like railway lines, was named by the British after a busy London rail interchange. It is generally thought that Bronze Age (2000–1000BC) people made them with some kind of non-wheeled vehicles, but there are other hypotheses, including one that attributes them to the Carthaginians and their iron-rimmed wheeled carts. The ruts vary in depth (40–60cm/15–24in) and width, which gives credence to the idea that they were created by wooden sleds made of tree trunks, tipped with iron runners, and used to transport a variety of heavy goods and materials.

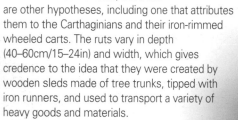

Cart ruts are found in various places in Malta and Gozo, but the largest concentration can be found here at Clapham Junction. The cart ruts are signposted, but when you reach the site it takes a few minutes to establish their presence. Once they are identified they take on an air of mystery. Why are they in this particular location, why do they converge, why do some disappear over the cliff edge and why are there so many of them?

✚ F4 ✉ 500m (550yds) south of Buskett Gardens
✋ Free 🚌 81

DINGLI CLIFFS

The village of Dingli, 253m (830ft) above sea level, is the highest on Malta and the nearby Dingli Cliffs offer one of the island's most stunning panoramic views. The Mediterranean appears as a vast expanse with the islet of Filfla lost out on its own. On the edge of the cliff stands the tiny and lonely chapel of St Magdalena, dating back to 1646. Most visitors arrive in their own transport (although a bus serves Dingli village and it is a short walk to the cliffs), but the location can only really be appreciated by leaving your vehicle and taking a stroll.

✚ E4 ✉ 15km (9 miles) southwest of Valletta, 4km (2.5 miles) south of Rabat 🍴 Bobbyland Bar and Restaurant (➤ 114) 🚌 81

ĦAĠAR QIM AND MNAJDRA
Best places to see, ➤ 40–41.

ĦAL SAFLIENI HYPOGEUM
Best places to see, ➤ 42–43.

MARSASKALA

The postcard-pretty harbour of Marsaskala (also spelt Marsascala) witnessed the last Turkish assault on Malta in 1614. Although the troops landed they were beaten back while heading inland and the Knights built a mighty fort on the nearby headland to deter any future visit. Today, a tourist infrastructure is developing quickly and Marsaskala welcomes visitors with open arms. Appropriately enough, part of the fort's location has been turned into the area's premier tourist hotel, the Corinthia Jerma Palace Hotel. The village of Marsaskala has an agreeable setting by the water's edge with plenty of cafés and good seafood restaurants overlooking the bay and its pastel-coloured boats. In recent years the nightlife scene has become increasingly popular with visitors and Maltese alike. Between them, the bars and discos and an up-to-date cinema and restaurant complex appeal across the age range.

There is no beach, but nearby St Thomas Bay, 1km (0.5 miles) to the south, has sandy banks and shallow water. In summer it can seem too busy, but it is easy to escape the crowds by heading south along the coast towards Delimara Point. The road to St Thomas Bay from Marsaskala passes Mamo Tower, a 17th-century tower with an interesting cruciform design and just one room with a vaulted roof. It was privately built by a landowner to deter slave-collecting expeditions from North Africa dropping in to St Thomas Bay and abducting his peasants.

✚ L4 ✉ 9km (5.5 miles) southeast of Valletta 🍴 Cafés and restaurants (€–€€) by the seafront 🚌 17, 19, 20, 22

MARSAXLOKK

Marsaxlokk is the largest fishing village on Malta, and the traditional and strong sense of community suggests it will remain so. Both the Turks, in 1565, and Napoleon, in 1798, landed their troops here and these days there is an annual summer invasion of tourists but Marsaxlokk retains its character and appeal. Each Sunday morning the quayside becomes an open-air fish market, and throughout the week the village's good seafood restaurants (➤ 114–116) serve the local catch.

There is no beach here, but interesting walks include a stroll to Delimara Point which passes a few bathing inlets on its eastern side. Heading south, a pleasant walk hugs the coastline as far as Birżebbuġa and takes in Għar Dalam along the way.

✚ L5 ✉ 10km (6 miles) southeast of Valletta
🍴 Cafés and restaurants (€–€€) by the seafront
🚌 27, 427 from Valletta; 427 and 627 from Buġibba; 28 from Conspicua

QRENDI

This is the perfect village for those who like to seek out relatively obscure places of historical interest. The diminutive Church of St Catherine Tat-Torba is worth a visit if only to wonder at its unique facade. Another oddity, for Malta, is the octagonal Gwarena Tower, while to the south of the village there is a natural wonder known as Il-Maqluba. This huge hole in the soft limestone, some 100m (330ft) across and 50m (165ft) deep, was caused presumably by the collapse of a subterranean cave. This gave rise to an unflattering legend concerning the people of Qrendi: the inhabitants were so ungodly that they and their village were cast into hell, via Il-Maqluba, but even the devil rejected them and the tangled mass was cast into the sea thus creating the islet of Filfla.

✚ H5 ✉ 11km (7 miles) southwest of Valletta 🍴 A few bars (€) 🚌 35, 138; 350 from Mqabba

SIĠĠIEWI

This village, one of 10 original parishes, had a population of 1,500 when the Knights arrived in 1530. It has one of the foremost baroque churches on the island. The dominating Church of St Nicholas was built in the last quarter of the 17th century with two aisles and a dome added in the 19th century. The richly embellished interior includes an altarpiece that is the last, unfinished, work by Mattia Preti.

Under 5km (3 miles) to the west of Siġġiewi the attractively located Inquisitor's Summer Palace, built in 1625 by Inquisitor Visconti, may be viewed, but not visited as it is now a summer home for the prime minister. Some 4km (2.5 miles) to the south of Siġġiewi, on the coast, is Għar Lapsi. There is no sand but it is a popular swimming spot with Maltese families and there is a footpath to the Blue Grotto (➤ 102–103).

🚩 G4 ✉ 8km (5 miles) southwest of Valletta 🍴 A bar (€) in Siġġiewi serves snacks and there is a restaurant (€) at Għar Lapsi 🚌 89, 94

TARXIEN TEMPLES

Best places to see, ➤ 54–55.

VERDALA PALACE

This castle-like palace was built in 1586 by a Grandmaster as a summer residence and now, as a seasonal home for the president, performs a similar kind of function. It has been renovated and enriched over the centuries but the luxury of its interior cannot be seen by visitors unless it once again opens to the public on certain days of the week.

🚩 F4 ✉ 3km (2 miles) southeast of Rabat 🚌 81

ŻABBAR

The Turks set up camp here on the dawn of the Great Siege, when the then village lay just outside the later Cottonera Lines, the fortified walls protecting the Three Cities, where the Knights first settled. When the French were blockaded behind the Lines in 1800, Żabbar became the focus for the Maltese military opposition. French cannon fire did serious damage to the Church of Our Lady of Graces but the restored church is worth a visit. Originally designed by Tommaso Dingli in 1640, the impressive ceiling of the nave is his only intact work. The exterior facade is a good example of over-the-top baroque. On Sunday mornings the church opens a small ecclesiastical museum with a number of votive paintings. East of town the Hompesch Arch, which is forlornly placed in the middle of a road junction, is a sad reminder of Malta's last Grandmaster, who surrendered to Napoleon.

✚ K4 ✉ 7km (4 miles) southeast of Valletta ☎ 21824383 (church museum) 🕐 Sun 9–12 (church museum) 🖐 Free (church museum) 🍴 Apart from a café (€) at the end of Santiwarju Street near the church, there is not much choice 🚌 18, 19, 21, 22, 23; 17 from Valletta; 300 from Senglea

ŻEBBUĠ

Żebbuġ, one of the original 10 parishes of 1486, is indifferent to tourism and few visitors bother stopping other than those seeking out interesting old churches. The Church of St Philip, built in 1632 in the town square, is the most impressive place of worship, designed by the son of the famous Gerolamo Cassar, who was so influential in the building of Valletta. There are similarities with St John's Co-Cathedral (▶ 48–49). More difficult to find is the tiny Church of Tal-Ħlas, tucked away to the north of the town centre, worth seeking out for its barred iron windows in the facade. This useful feature protected the priest during pirate raids, while he said Mass for his much less fortunate parishioners outside.

✚ G4 ✉ 8km (5 miles) southwest of Valletta 🍴 Nowhere suitable for a meal 🚌 88

ŻEJTUN

Roman and Punic remains have been unearthed in Żejtun but the chief reason for visiting this old town, one of the 10 original parishes, lies with its two fine churches. On an island site the baroque **Church of St Catherine,** a massively solid composition in stone, is regarded as the best example of Lorenzo Gafà's style. Some, though, may prefer the smaller Church of St Gregory, a few minutes' walk away and close to the restful Luqa Briffa Gardens.

St Gregory's, one of the best of the island's older churches, was medieval but in the 16th century the Knights made structural alterations and now only the nave and facade remain of the original building. In 1969, secret wall passages revealed dozens of skeletons.

✚ K5 ✉ 7km (4 miles) southeast of Valletta

Church of St Catherine

🕐 Mon–Fri 7am–8am, Sat 6:30am–7:30am, Sun 8am–9am, 11–noon 🍴 Café (€) is signposted from the square near St Catherine's 🚌 27, 29, 30

ŻURRIEQ

This market town, one of the 10 original parishes, is usually just passed through en route to the Blue Grotto or Ħaġar Qim, but there are two interesting churches. The exterior of the Church of St Catherine is not exceptional but inside there are paintings by Mattia Preti, done by the artist when he fled here to escape a plague in 1675.

Just 1km (0.5 miles) west of Żurrieq, off the road to the Blue Grotto, and in a deserted medieval settlement, is the delightful **Ħal-Millieri Church of the Annunciation.** This chapel was built by farmers in 1420, abandoned in the 17th century, and rediscovered and renovated in the 1960s. The 15th-century frescoes depicting the saints are unique on Malta; the church has a wonderfully antique atmosphere and is utterly different in spirit from the usual baroque ecclesiastical edifices.

✚ J5 ✉ 9km (5.5 miles) south of Valletta

Ħal-Millieri Church of the Annunciation

☎ 21225952; www.dinlarthelwa.org (National Trust, in charge of Ħal Millieri church) 🕐 First Sunday of the month 9–noon 🍴 Cafés and restaurants (€) 🚌 32, 34, 38, 138

HOTELS

BIRŻEBBUĠA
Seabreeze Hotel (€)
This family-owned small hotel is a good find for budget-conscious visitors. Set across from the beach at Pretty Bay, it's well located for attractions in the south. The hotel offers an on-site restaurant, bar, games room and lounge. It's a boxy building and the rooms are simply furnished, but certainly value for money.

✉ Pretty Bay ☎ 21651256

MARSASKALA
Cerviola Hotel (€)
A comfortable, three-star, four-storey hotel with a good range of amenities including a sizeable rooftop pool and sun deck. The Cerviola has a restaurant and bar and offers free safe-deposit facilities in reception. Rooms have en-suite shower rooms, fridge and TV.

✉ Triq il-Qaliet ☎ 21632761 (freephone from the UK 0800 0152797); www.cerviolahotel.com

RESTAURANTS

DINGLI CLIFFS
Bobbyland Bar and Restaurant (€)
A landmark restaurant which is not easily missed if you turn to the right after arriving at Dingli Cliffs (➤ 104–105) from Rabat. Best off season for a quieter meal. Excellent food from meat dishes to fresh fish.

✉ Panoramic Road, Dingli Cliffs ☎ 21452895 🕒 Tue–Fri 11:30–2:30, 7–10:30, Sat 11:30–2, 7–10:30, Sun 11:30–2:15, 7–10 🚌 81

MARSASKALA
Al Kafe (€)
A pleasant pizzeria and cafeteria with a prime location on the waterfront and tables filling the pavement under giant umbrellas.

✉ Marina Street, Marsaskala ☎ 21632282 🕒 Mar–Dec daily 10:30–11. Closed Jan–Feb 🚌 19, 22

Grabiel (€€€)

Probably the most popular restaurant with local people, Grabiel is presided over by its eccentric and colourful owner/chef. The menu changes regularly but always includes meat dishes plus tasty, locally caught fresh fish. Right in the centre of town.

✉ Mifsud Bonnici Square ☎ 21684194 🕓 Mon–Sat noon–2, 5–midnight. Closed 14–28 Aug 🚌 19, 22

Jakarta (€€)

Offers a menu of oriental dishes. There is a set meal for two people besides the à-la-carte choices, which includes satay, spare-ribs and crispy duck with pancakes.

✉ Triq Tal-Gardiel ☎ 21633993 🕓 Tue–Sun 7–11, Sun noon–2pm 🚌 19, 20

Tal-Familja (€€)

Past the Sun City cinema, this is a large restaurant with outdoor tables available. The fish and local dishes are likely to be the best items on the menu, and vegetarians are catered for.

✉ Triq il-Gardiel ☎ 21632161 🕓 Tue–Sun 12–5, 6:30pm–2am

MARSAXLOKK

Hunter's Tower (€€)

This restaurant has been open for over 30 years and has grown into a large operation, with plenty of space in the main dining room and the shady garden. The menu concentrates on fresh fish, but is supplemented by pizzas and Maltese dishes.

✉ Wilga Street ☎ 21651792; www.hunterstower.com 🕓 21 Sep–21 Jun Tue–Thu 11:30–3, Fri–Sat 6:30–11; 22 Jun–20 Sep Tue–Thu 6:30–11, Fri–Sun 11:30–3, 6:30–11. Closed Mon

Ir-Rizzu (€€)

See page 59.

Is-Sajjied Bar & Restaurant (€€)

Good views of the sea, which is where the best dishes on the restaurant's menu are caught. There are other Italian-style dishes available plus an extensive wine list.

⊠ Xatt is-Sajjieda ☎ 21652549 ⊕ Daily 12–2:30, 7–10:30. Closed Sat lunch, Sun dinner, Mon ▣ 19, 22

SHOPPING

Marsaxlokk open-air market

Basically a fish market, where the variety of shapes and colours of the Mediterranean fish here is surprising. Many of them end up on the local restaurants' plates. It attracts people from all over the island.

⊠ Along the waterfront, Marsaxlokk ⊕ Sun 7am–11:30am ▣ 27 from Valletta; 427 from Buġibba; 627 from Paceville

ENTERTAINMENT

The south isn't renowned for its nightlife, and the action centres around a few bars in the resorts.

BIRŻEBBUĠĠA

Cherry's Bar

Set in a period mansion, Cherry's attracts young locals for a drink and a game of pool.

⊠ Pretty Bay ☎ 21651072 ⊕ Mon–Thu and Sun 6pm–11pm, Fri 4pm–midnight, Sat noon–midnight

MARSAXLOKK

Jumpin Jak's

With juke box or guest DJ there's plenty of music here, plus darts, pool and live football screened for those who just can't miss it.

⊠ Triq il-Qaliet ☎ 21634173 ⊕ Mon–Sat 7pm–midnight, Sun noon–midnight

ŻABBAR

Crazy Horse Bar

Small local bar catering for a more mature crowd of regulars.

⊠ 228 Sanctuary Street ☎ 99458977 (mobile) ⊕ Daily 11–11

Central Malta

The diverse centre of the island encompasses Malta's biggest, most popular and most concentrated holiday playground.

Sliema and St Julian's; the 'three villages' of Attard, Balzan and Lija, once home to the wealthy elite and still an exclusive enclave; and, rising above the confusion, the ancient city of Mdina, Malta's capital before Valetta was built, surrounded by sturdy walls that insulate it from the cacophony of sound that engulfs much of the island, and bursting with history and atmosphere.

MDINA AND RABAT

High ground away from the coast made Mdina a natural site for a defensively minded community, and Bronze Age people were probably the first to settle here. The Phoenicians and Romans knew it respectively as Maleth and Melita, and the Arabs built walls 19m (62ft) high around the town they called Mdina, leaving the poorer people outside in Rabat. In the following centuries Mdina emerged as the island's capital until the Knights made Valletta the new capital in 1571. Today, fortified medieval Mdina and Rabat should not be missed by any first-time visitor. Mdina's honey-coloured walls and narrow winding alleyways and Rabat's catacombs and Roman remains make any visit memorable.

✚ Mdina – F3; Rabat – F3

Magazine Street and Greek's Gate

Magazine Street, so called because munitions were once stored here, borders the western side of Mdina and, unless a tour group has arrived, there is a surprising air of tranquillity to the place. There are many fine details to appreciate in the old dwellings, and photographers, if the light allows, enjoy trying to capture in close-up the brass knockers, the cut stone or the window mouldings. Greek's Gate is named after a small number of Greeks who came to Malta with the Knights from Rhodes and settled in this corner of Mdina. The walls of

Greek's Gate are very old, dating back to Arab times. Just north of Greek's Gate is another breach in the wall, made in the 19th century for those travelling to Mdina by train. The old train station, now a restaurant, can be seen in the valley below.

🍴 Cafés and restaurants (€–€€) in Mdina and Rabat 🚌 80, 81, 82, 84 from Valletta; 65 from Sliema and Valletta; 86 from Buġibba

Malta Aviation Museum

Suitably located at Malta's historic World War II airport. The Spitfire and Dakota are two of the prized exhibits. You will also find a good crafts village with stalls in the original RAF Nissen huts.

✉ Hut 13, Crafts Village, Ta' Qali ☎ 21416095; www.maltaaviationmuseum.com 🕐 Daily 9–5 ✋ Moderate

Domus Romana

Remains of a Roman town house were discovered just outside Mdina in 1881 and the museum is built over the site. For anyone interested in ancient Rome there are some interesting exhibits. Downstairs these include some of the original mosaics that once adorned a floor in the house, surrounded by remains of columns and busts unearthed in different corners of Malta. Noteworthy exhibits in the main gallery include an olive crusher, discovered at Marsaxlokk, once used to extract the pips so that oil could be made from the pulp. There is also a 2nd-century tombstone recording the death of a comedian and musician and various smaller finds.

✉ Wesgha Tal-Muzew, Rabat
☎ 21454125 ⏱ Daily 9–5 ✋ Moderate

Palazzo Falson

When Malta was under Spanish rule, the Maltese nobility emulated the architecture of the Sicilian nobility (also under Spanish rule) in their fine homes. This style, known as Siculo-Norman, is best represented by the Palazzo Falson, in the design of the windows and the moulding – most

notably over the two doorways. The mansion has been fully restored and furnished in 16th- to 17th-century style with over 3,500 objects. There are free audio-guides to help you get the most out of your visit.

✉ Triq Villegaignon, Mdina ☎ 21454512
🕐 Tue–Sun 10–5 ✋ No entrance fee but a donation is welcomed

Palazzo Santa Sophia

The date plaque of 1233 makes this the oldest building in Mdina. The ground floor is authentically medieval but the first floor, still true to the Siculo-Norman style, was added in 1938. Look up to the first-floor level and you can see the typical horizontal moulded design known as a 'string course'. Across the road is the tiny church of St Roque, dedicated to the patron saint of diseases, which originally stood close to Mdina Gate. Grandmaster de Vilhena probably did not like the idea of a church that attracted the sick set so close to his residence, Palazzo Vilhena, so he had the first church taken apart and a new one built here.

A little further up the road on the other side is the Carmelite Church. The building is not architecturally significant, but it does however possess some historical worth in the story of the 1798 revolt against France, which took place after the French confiscated valuable property from the church.

✉ Triq Villegaignon, Mdina

Palazzo Vilhena/National Museum of Natural History

The magnificent Palazzo Vilhena, also known as the Magisterial Palace, was built by the Grandmaster de Vilhena in the early 18th century. With a central courtyard, it was originally intended as his private residence. It later became an administrative building and the rear was turned into law courts, which in turn led to the basements being converted into a prison. The underground space has now been converted again to house the Mdina Dungeons (► 72). At the beginning of the 20th century the British turned the main building into a sanatorium, which it remained until the 1950s. It now houses the National Museum of Natural History.

✉ St Publius Square, on the right immediately after passing through Mdina Gate ☎ 21455951 (Museum of Natural History) 🕐 Daily 9–5 💷 Inexpensive

St Paul's Cathedral

Best places to see, ► 52–53.

St Paul's Church and St Paul's Grotto

The original church on this site was built in 1572 but most of what you now see belongs to the late 17th century, when it was remodelled by Lorenzo Gafà after an earthquake destroyed its predecessor. The features worth noting include the altarpiece, designed by Mattia Preti, and the paintings, among which is *The Shipwreck of St Paul* by Stefano Erardi. Underneath the church is a grotto that would be unremarkable save for the legend that St Paul found shelter in this place after his shipwreck; the marble statue of St Paul has therefore become an important place of pilgrimage.

✉ Pjazza Tal-Parocca, Rabat ☎ 21454467 🕐 Daily 9:30–1:30, 2:30–5 ✋ Free

St Paul's and St Agatha's Catacombs
Best places to see, ➤ 50–51.

Tales of the Silent City, Medieval Times and the Knights of Malta
These multimedia shows and exhibitions, in *palazzos* along Villegaignon and Magazine streets, bring to life the history and lore of Mdina, from its origins to the present day.

The **Knights of Malta** exhibition houses about 120 life-sized figures and is available in many languages.

Tales of the Silent City
✉ Palazzo Gatto Murina
☎ 21451179 🕐 Daily 9:30–4:30
✋ Moderate

Medieval Times
✉ Palazzo Notabile
☎ 21454625
🕐 Mon–Sat 9:30–9:30
✋ Moderate

Knights of Malta
✉ Casa Magazzini
☎ 21451342 🕐 Mon–Fri 10:30–4 ✋ Moderate

a walk around Mdina

The walk begins at the Mdina Gate, built in 1724 by Grandmaster de Vilhena. Immediately after passing through the gate the Mdina Dungeons (▶ 72), a gruesome museum, is on the right. Next door is the Palazzo Vilhena and the National Museum of Natural History (▶ 122).

Take the first left and stay on this street, Triq Villegaignon, immediately passing Inguanez Street. A little way on brings you into Pjazza San Pawl, St Paul's

Square, with a large church bearing two clocks (one of which tells the correct time; the other is there to confuse the devil). Continue along Triq Villegaignon, past several shops, and turn left into the narrow St Peter's Street. At the bottom, turn right into Magazine Street.

Walking along Magazine Street (► 119), you will pass the Knights of Malta exhibition (► 123), with its neat little café. There are views from the terrace here and more alfresco places up ahead which are worth a stop.

After passing a second tea garden, walk into Bastion Square where there are views from the ramparts and places to enjoy a rest and a drink. Take the first right turning into Triq Villegaignon.

At the top end of Triq Villegaignon, you first pass Palazzo Falson (► 120-121) and then Medieval Times (► 123).

Take the first left after Palazzo Notabile into the narrow St Roque Street and at the T-junction, at the bottom of the street, go left into Bastion Street and pass the entrance to Fontanella Café. Go left, take the first left into Our Savior Street and follow this street until, turning left at the T-junction, you are back on Triq Villegaignon, Mdina's main street, which leads back to the starting point of the walk.

Distance 1km (0.5 miles)
Time 2–4 hours, depending on visits
Start/end point Mdina Gate
🚌 80, 81, 84, 86 from Valletta; 86 from Buġibba; 65 from Sliema;
Lunch Fontanella Tea Garden (► 149)

DAN IL-KURĊIFISS JURI L-POST FEJN
KIENET TINGĦATA L-FORKA FI ŻMIEN
L-ORDNI TA SAN GWANN.
FIS-SEKLU 16.

THIS STONE CRUCIFIX MARKS THE 16th.
CENTURY SITE OF PUBLIC EXECUTIONS
HELD AT THE TIME OF THE
ORDER OF ST. JOHN.

VITTORIOSA

In 1530 the Knights of the Order of St John chose a settlement on a narrow peninsula of land overlooking the creeks of the Grand Harbour as their headquarters, and set about fortifying it. Then known as Birgu, in 1565 the town was besieged for three months by the Turks and, though many lives were lost, the town was not taken. After the siege the Knights began the construction of a new capital but Birgu was given the name Vittoriosa – the victorious one – as an accolade. Many of the early buildings and fortifications of the Knights are still here along with narrow winding streets, and there are many reminders of the second great siege during World War II. ✚ K3

Church of St Lawrence

Originally built in the 11th century, this historically important church was rebuilt in 1530 by the Knights of St John as their Conventual Church. In 1691 it was virtually reconstructed by Lorenzo Gafà (builder of the cathedrals at Mdina and Victoria on Gozo) in the baroque style. The well-balanced and impressive exterior with twin clock towers and dome is matched by a lavish dimly lit interior. The church was damaged during World War II but the reconstruction and repairs are faithful to the original. Red marble and frescoes by Cortis and Joseph Calli adorn the walls and the ceiling. The most important work displayed in the chapel is a depiction of the martyrdom of St Lawrence by Mattia Preti.

✉ Triq San Lawrenz ☎ 21827057 🕒 Daily 6–10, 4–7 ✋ Free 🍴 Café Riche (▶ 151) 🚌 1, 2, 4, 6 ❓ Festival of St Lawrence, 10 Aug

Fort St Angelo

Records show that a fort called Castrum Maris stood on the site of Fort Angelo in 1274, but it is believed that a building was here long before that, possibly a temple to the Phoenician goddess Asthart. In 1530 it became the seat of the Grandmaster and the Knights added more fortifications, which withstood the Great Siege. When the siege ended the great bell was rung continuously for a day. Later the fort became a prison where rebellious Knights were held.

There are two chapels inside the fortress, one a 12th-century building dedicated to the Virgin Mary and the other from the 16th-century, devoted to St Anne. The early Grandmasters are buried

here, as are many of the Knights who died defending the city.
The fort was the British naval headquarters and the base for Allied
naval operations in the Mediterranean during World War II.

✉ Vittoriosa Wharf 🍽 Café Riche (➤ 151) 🚌 1, 2, 4, 6

The Inquisitor's Palace

This building began its life in the Norman period as the Court of
Justice but was enlarged and taken over when the Papal
Inquisition came to Malta in 1574. The 62 Inquisitors sat here and
an unknown number of people were tortured and died at their
hands. Two of the Inquisitors went on to become popes,
Alexander VII and Innocent XII. In the museum are exhibits of
household utensils, tools, furniture and craft paraphernalia.
The dungeons with prisoners' graffiti are still there, as are the
courtrooms and the Inquisitors' chapel. One wing of the building
dates back to the original Norman structure.

✉ Main Gate Street ☎ 21827006 🕐 Daily 9–5 ♿ Expensive 🍽 Café
Riche (➤ 151) 🚌 1, 2, 4, 6

The Maritime Museum

The walls of the Maritime Museum are decorated with pictures of
the hundreds of ships which have played a part in Malta's past
while the various rooms effectively display different eras in naval
history. On display there are Roman anchors, models of the ships
of the Order of St John and Royal Navy vessels, as well as

medieval navigating equipment,
cannons, ancient uniforms and
models of the tiny *luzzu* (fishing
boats) which can still be seen
bobbing about the harbour.

✉ Vittoriosa Wharf ☎ 21660052
🕐 Daily 9–5 ♿ Moderate 🍽 Café
Riche (➤ 151) 🚌 1, 2, 4, 6

St Joseph's Oratory

This tiny, interesting museum is set in a little square outside the north door of the Church of St Lawrence. Exhibits include the hat and sword worn by Grandmaster la Vallette, and curiosities ranging from long wafer-holding tongs used by the priests to give communion when there was a plague, an ancient crucifix used at public executions, and an early Bible used by the Inquisitors, to a much-used pack of playing cards of 1609.

✉ Vittoriosa Square 🕐 Mon–Sat 8:30–12, 2–4, Sun 9:30–12 ✋ Free 🍴 Café Riche (➤ 151) 🚌 1, 2, 4, 6

Victory Square

This square was the centre of social life here in Vittoriosa for centuries. In it is the Victory Monument, erected in 1705, a statue of St Lawrence and a stone crucifix marking the spot where executions took place. On 10 August this square comes alive at the Festival of St Lawrence. Around the square are the *auberges* of Germany, England (which never moved to Valletta because of the Reformation) and Auvergne, but these *auberges* are modest compared to the grand ones in Valletta.

✉ Vittoriosa Square 🍴 Café Riche (➤ 151) 🚌 1, 2, 4, 6

Vittoriosa 1565 Museum

This museum is a celebration of the 1565 siege depicting Turks scaling walls and brave Knights defending their city.

✉ 24 Wenzu Dyer Street ☎ 21891565 🕐 Sep–Jun Mon–Sat 9–4, Sun 9–1; Aug Mon–Sat 9–2, Sun 9–1 ✋ Moderate 🍴 Café Riche (➤ 151)

a walk in Vittoriosa

The old capital has both impressive sites and tiny, homely stores and shops on this important promontory in Grand Harbour.

Enter Vittoriosa through the main gate, the Gate of Provence, which leads directly to the main street, Triq il-Mina il-Kbira.

On the right the Inquisitor's Palace (➤ 129) is passed and soon after the street enters Victory Square (➤ 130).

Keep on your left for St Joseph's Oratory (➤ 130) and take the nearby turning out of the Square on Triq Nestu Laiviera and down the stepped pavement for the Church of St Lawrence (➤ 126).

With your back to the church entrance, turn right at the water's edge and pass through the gate, pausing to admire the splendid Canaletto-like view across the water.

Passing the Maritime Museum (➤ 129) on the right, walk along the quayside past the boats and ships and cross the small bridge at the end before walking up the broad ramp to Fort St Angelo (➤ 128–129).

Stop to admire the views on both sides and maybe take a photograph.

Retrace your steps to Victory Square and, from the position where you first entered the Square along Triq il-Kbira, take the narrow turning in the right corner (which has a street sign saying Block 5).

The *auberges* (none open) were the first, more humble ones of the Order. Go straight down this narrow lane, passing the Auberge d'Angleterre on the right.

At the end turn right and follow the street uphill until a fork is reached. Bear to the right and go along this street, Pacifiku Scicluna, to the end where you turn right at the T-junction. Then take the next left to enter once more the main street, Triq il-Kbira, which leads back to the gate where you entered Vittoriosa. Café Riche is on the left after leaving through the gate.

Distance 1.5km (1 mile)
Time 2–4 hours, depending on church and museum visits
Start/end point Main gate entrance to Vittoriosa 🚌 1, 2, 4, 6
Lunch 🍴 Café Riche (➤ 151)
❓ A tourist board brochure, *A Walking Tour of the Cottonera*, includes a map of Vittoriosa

More to see in Central Malta

ATTARD

Attard and the neighbouring villages of Balzan and Lija (see opposite) are known collectively as the Three Villages, but it is Attard that has the chief claim to fame. Historically, it is associated with the 17th-century Grandmaster Antoine de Paule, a hedonist who is infamously linked with the decline of the Order of St John into decadence. His summer residence near Attard, San Anton Palace, is now the official residence of Malta's president.

Although its interior cannot be visited, the San Anton Gardens are open to the public. In Attard itself St Mary's Church is a splendid example of Renaissance church architecture, designed by Tommaso Dingli when he was only 22 years old.

✚ G3 ✉ 7km (4 miles) southwest of Valletta 🍴 Villa Corinthia Restaurant (➤ 148) 🚌 40, 80, 81, 82, 84, 810

BALZAN AND LIJA

These two adjoining villages, just a short walk north of Attard, are of interest principally because of their churches. In Balzan the Church of the Annunciation and the Church of St Roque, dating back to the late 16th century, are both well preserved. Lija's Church of St Saviour looks uninspiring from the outside, but on a Sunday morning the late 17th-century painted interior can be appreciated. A 10-minute walk away in St Saviour Street is the Tal-Mirakli Church (Our Lady of Miracles), said to be sited in the exact geographical centre of Malta. It was rebuilt in the 17th century and has a fine altarpiece by Mattia Preti.

✚ H3 ✉ 7km (4 miles) southwest of Valletta 🍴 The Old Smuggler (€), 36 Main Street, Balzan 🚌 40, 59, 73, 153, 159

BIRKIRKARA

Visitors tend to just drive through the urban sprawl of Birkirkara and indeed from the window of a vehicle it does not seem very inviting. Among the numerous churches is the Collegiate Church of St Helen, the largest on Malta and a notable example of ecclesiastical baroque architecture. The exterior has a striking facade and entablature while inside are some beautiful and graceful frescoes. In the older part of town there is still a lot of character in the confusing maze of streets and houses.

✚ H3 ✉ 6km (4 miles) southwest of Valletta 🍴 Better to eat in Attard or Lija 🚌 Numerous routes including 19, 40, 42, 47 and 52–59

GĦARGĦUR

This small village, subdued and picturesque, is hidden away at the top of a ridge, and manages unintentionally to evoke a sense of Malta's medieval past. If you are driving from Valletta, the turning off the main road is signposted for Madliena just before the Splash & Fun Park (➤ 73). The uphill trip to Għargħur is like a journey into the sealed-off past as the road winds its way over an old viaduct and up into the sun-baked countryside. One of the town's features, the **Church of St Bartholomew** was designed by the architect Tommaso Dingli in 1636 and its gloomy interior does little to detract from Għargħur's air of antiquity.

Għargħur marks the northern end of the Victoria Lines (➤ 143) and nearby Fort Madliena is part of this defensive system. From Għargħur you can either take a walk or drive inland to enjoy the spectacular scenery of the indented coastline, as well as impressive views of the Great Fault that cuts off this corner of Malta.

✚ H2

Church of St Bartholomew

✉ 7km (4 miles) northwest of Valletta 🕓 Mon–Sat 4–7:30, Sun 6–11:30, 4–7:30 🍴 Madliena Cottage Bar and Restaurant 🚌 55

GRAND HARBOUR

Best places to see, ➤ 38–39.

MANOEL ISLAND

Connected to the mainland by a bridge, Manoel Island has an unfortunate history. The Knights of Malta used the island as a quarantine station during plagues, when it eventually could deal with up to 1,000 people at a time. The British used it as a hospital until 1940, when it became a submarine base. Heavy bombing during World War II took its toll on Fort Manoel, which was constructed in 1732 to guard **Marsamxett Harbour.** Manoel Island is currently under redevelopment and the historic buildings are being renovated as part of a mixed-use residential and tourist area that will include a marina and a 5-star hotel.

✚ J3

Marsamxett Harbour

✉ Between Sliema and Valletta 🍴 Cafés and restaurants (€) close to mainland seafront 🚌 60, 61, 62 to Yacht Marina and then across the bridge

MOSTA

It is the immense parish church, the Mosta Rotunda, in this busy town in the centre of Malta that attracts visitors. The Rotunda, built in the mid-19th century, has massive walls up to 6m (20ft) deep and these allowed the enormous dome – the fourth largest in Europe – to be constructed without scaffolding. This amazing building feat, which lasted 27 years, was helped by the older church on the same site which was only dismantled when the new church was complete. Some question the aesthetic harmony of the two belfries and the Ionic columns of the facade fronting such a large dome, but this cannot detract from the beautiful interior, with six side chapels, intricate marble floor and almost three-dimensional murals by Giuseppe Calì. The sacristy contains a replica of a 200kg (440-pound) bomb that pierced the dome in 1942 but fortunately failed to explode amid the congregation. Two other bombs bounced off the dome without exploding.

✚ G3 ✉ 8km (5 miles) west of Valletta ☎ 21433826 ⏰ Daily 9–5, but not during religious services ♿ Free 🍴 Cafés and restaurants (€) near the church 🚌 43–45, 47, 49, 52, 56–59, 65, 86, 145, 153, 157–159, 427. Service 50 summer only, 52 mornings only

MSIDA

This once small fishing village set in a creek of Marsamxett Harbour developed into a thriving town, helped in 1989 by the building of a yacht marina, now part of Malta's main yachting marina. The parish church of St Joseph is worth a visit for its two altarpieces by Guiseppe Calì. The Ta'Xbiex Seafront, where yachts berth, offers pleasant views of Floriana across the water. There is a multitude of cafés to choose from where you can sit and watch the world go by.

✚ J3 ✉ 3km (2 miles) southwest of Valletta 🍽 Cafés and restaurants (€) in walking distance 🚌 40–45, 47, 49, 50, 52–64, 66–68, 141, 142, 145, 153, 169, 452, 499, 662, 667, 671. Service 52 and 54 mornings only, 50 summer only

NAXXAR

The parish of Naxxar, on a commanding site, dates back to 1436 so, while there may be some credence to the story that after his shipwreck St Paul came here and washed his clothes out (Naxxar translates as 'to hang clothes to dry'), one might wonder why he trekked 8km (5 miles) from the coast to do so. The quiet suburb of San Pawl tat-Tarġa ('St Paul of the Step'), where St Paul is said to have preached from the steps of the church, is only 1km (0.5 miles) away. **Palazzo Parisio,** in the central square, is open to the public. Built for Grandmaster de Vilhena, the *palazzo* serves to illustrate the lifestyle and dwelling conditions of the rich nobility in 19th-century Malta.

✚ G2 ✉ 9km (5.5 miles) west of Valletta 🍽 Bars and cafés (€) across the road from the church 🚌 54–56, 59, 65, 159

Palazzo Parisio

✉ Victory Square, Naxxar ☎ 21412461; www.palazzoparisio.com
🕐 Mon–Sat 9–6 (last admission 4:30) 👋 Expensive

QORMI

Too many visitors travel past Qormi on their way to
somewhere else, but they miss the town's impressive
medieval heritage, which is reflected in the maze of very
narrow streets and alleys in the old part of town, a little to the
north of the modern town centre. Qormi was once known as
Casal Fornaro, meaning 'Village of Bakers'. There are no
special sights to look out for, although the tall church of St
George is a pleasing edifice with a well-proportioned exterior
that balances its facade, spires and dome. This acts as a useful
landmark while exploring the nearby winding streets where
one is occasionally surprised by a lovely 16th-century house
with an ornate balcony.

✚ H4 ✉ 4km (2.5 miles) southwest of Valletta 🍴 Nowhere suitable
in the old part of town 🚌 88, 89 (outskirts only), 91

ST JULIAN'S, PACEVILLE AND ST GEORGE'S BAY

St Julian's was a sleepy fishing village that awoke one day in
1798 to find nearly 500 of Napoleon's ships in the bay. The
French invasion was largely unopposed and 200 years later a
different kind of invasion takes place each summer when
thousands of visitors of all nationalities visit. It is attractively
located along the line of the two curving bays of Balluta and
St Julian's (sometimes called Spinola) and its promenade is a
continuation of Tower Road in Sliema. A vast swathe of the
St Julian's coastline has been redeveloped as Portomaso –
an upmarket housing and marina complex with a selection
of shops, restaurants and hotels.

Going beyond St Julian's is a small promontory where
Paceville is located. Paceville (pronounced patch-e-ville) is the
nightlife capital of Malta and when darkness falls neon lights
illuminate the discos, pubs and cafés that jostle for space
and customers. The latest addition to the entertainment
scene is Bay Street, a modern complex of trendy shops,

cafés and restaurants, with a bowling alley and a multi-screen cinema complex nearby (➤ 72).

Around the headland of Dragonara Point is St George's Bay, the only local beach area and consequently very popular. The sandy part of the beach is minute and, although the number of bobbing boats makes any kind of water activity difficult, the setting is very attractive and there are lidos near by. The far side of St George's Bay is developing into a mass of top-notch hotels, which are dominated by the San Gorg hotel, and there is a number of quality restaurants.

✚ J2 ✉ 7km (4 miles) northwest of Valletta 🍴 Plenty of cafés and restaurants (€–€€€) in the area 🚌 62, 64–68, 70, 164, 667, 671 from Valletta; 627 from Buġibba; 645 and 652 from Sliema

SENGLEA

Senglea, on a peninsula separating two waterways, is one of the historic Three Cities, along with Vittoriosa and Cospicua, where the Knights first settled after 1530. It was almost completely destroyed in World War II. The Safe Haven Gardens at the promontory's tip, the northern end of Victory Street, are worth a visit. From the lookout in the gardens there is a truly spectacular view of the Grand Harbour (➤ 38–39) with Vittoriosa's Fort St Angelo to the right and Valletta's mighty walls straight across the water. The stone vedette at the tip carries a sculptured eye and ear, symbols of vigilance.

✚ K3 ✉ 4km (2.5 miles) by road, south of Valletta

🍴 Café (€) near the church, but consider a picnic 🚌 3

SLIEMA

Sliema is an affluent and fashionable residential area for the Maltese and a prime holiday base for tourists thanks to a number of top- and middle-range hotels (➤ 147). Tower Road is its 5km (3-mile) promenade, full of shops and restaurants, and the road continues north to St Julian's and Paceville. There are no sandy beaches, but swimming and bathing off the rocky platforms along Tower Road is popular and there is a lido further along the road. The southern end of Tower Road joins The Strand, which fronts Sliema Creek. A short way along The Strand, at a transport point known as The Ferries, there is a bus terminus, a regular 5-minute ferry service to Valletta, Captain Morgan cruises to Comino and elsewhere (➤ 154) and, further down the road, the bridge to Manoel Island (➤ 137). The side streets into residential Sliema do not lead to any specific sights, but a meandering walk passes some fine villas built by the Maltese bourgeoisie in the early 20th century.

The Tigne headland offered the best point for guarding Marsamxett Harbour and Valletta, although the Knights did not build a fort here until 1792. The headland is currently part of a redevelopment project designed to mix the historical fortifications with modern waterside residential and office space.

✚ J3 ✉ 7km (4 miles) from Valletta 🍴 Restaurants and cafés (€–€€) 🚌 63, 65 from Valletta to Sliema ferries, 62–64, 66–68, 622, 671 from Valletta; 70, 627, 662 from Buġibba; 645 from Ċirkewwa; 65 from Mdina/Rabat; 652 from Golden Bay
🛥 Valletta–Sliema ferry (☎ 23463333)

VICTORIA LINES

There is a natural fault line running across Malta, the Great Fault, and the Knights were the first to capitalize on the defensive capabilities of this rift in the land that reaches 239m (785ft). They built watchtowers in gaps in the fault and later the British reinforced these, added more, and linked them up with a stonework parapet before officially christening them the Victoria Lines. Given their commanding position, the Victoria Lines offer scenic views across to Gozo and a focus for short walks in Malta's countryside. A recommended 3km (2-mile) stretch is that between Nadur (west of Rabat) and Falka Gap, and the Lines can also be reached from Għargħur, Mġarr, Mosta and Naxxar.

✚ G2 ✉ From Fomm ir-Riħ (southwest of Mġarr) to Fort Madliena (northeast of Għargħur) 🍴 Bring a picnic or eat in Mġarr, Mosta or Naxxar (€–€€) 🚌 47, 52 to Mġarr; 49, 53, 56, 58, 65, 145, 159 to Mosta; 55 to Għargħur and Naxxar

a drive

⨀around the north coast

The north coast was where St Paul was shipwrecked and where both the Turks and Napoleon landed.

Follow Tower Road in Sliema in the direction of St Julian's, following the signs for St Paul's Bay and Mellieħa.

Once outside the town the first stopping point is the unsignposted village of Għargħur (➤ 136).

To reach it, turn left at the turning for Madliena, which is signposted (if you pass Splash & Fun Park you have gone too far) and follow the road up to Għargħur.

Soak up the atmosphere of this ancient elevated village with its fine views.

*Retrace your route to the main road and turn left to
continue travelling west towards St Paul's Bay.*

The road hugs the coast as far as Salina Bay before
reaching Buġibba (➤ 160) and St Paul's Bay (➤ 160–161).
A walk along the promenade in St Paul's should give you
an appetite for lunch.

*After lunch drive the short distance further west to
Mellieħa (➤ 158), stopping perhaps at the island's
largest sandy beach which is just 2km (1.2 miles) north
of the town, descending the ridge. From the beach
continue to the northwest corner of Malta, the Marfa
Ridge, and photogenic Ċirkewwa, from where the
ferries depart for Gozo.*

There are several small beaches near here which, outside
weekends, attract few visitors.

*From Ċirkewwa head back to
Mellieħa and turn right at
the main roundabout to head
south to Għajn Tuffieħa
(➤ 156–157). From here take
the main road to Żebbieħ,
Mosta (➤ 138) and Naxxar
(➤ 139). From Naxxar it is a
short way back to Sliema.*

Distance 40km (25 miles)
Time 6–8 hours
Start/end point Sliema ✚ J3
Lunch Gillieru Restaurant, St Paul's
Bay (➤ 58)

HOTELS

BALZAN
Corinthia Palace Hotel and Spa (€€€)
One of the top hotels in Malta and well equipped. It offers a state-of-the-art health spa, indoor and outdoor pools and tennis and squash courts. There is also a courtesy bus to Valletta.

✉ De Paule Avenue ☎ 21440301; www.corinthiahotels.com 🚌 40

RABAT
Point de Vue (€)
This family-run budget guest house is in a 17th-century building. The location is central, just outside Mdina Gate, and some of the rooms offer a balcony as well as picturesque country views.

✉ 5 Saqqaja Square ☎ 21454117; www.pointdevuemalta.com 🚌 80, 81, 83, 84, 86, 65

ST JULIAN'S, PACEVILLE AND ST GEORGE'S BAY
Corinthia Hotel (€€€)
The St George's Bay area is being developed as an accommodation centre and this hotel holds pride of place. All 250 rooms on the six floors have a balcony and sea view. Great water and spa facilities.

✉ St George's Bay, St Julian's ☎ 21374114; www.corinthiahotels.com
🚌 62, 64–68, 70, 164, 667, 671 from Valletta; 627 from Buġibba; 645, 652 from Sliema

Hotel Valentina (€–€€)
The beautifully styled contemporary interior contrasts with the period facade at the Valentina. Rooms are spacious and furnished with clean Scandinavian lines accented by bold strokes of colour on walls and soft furnishings. Certainly a top-class B&B style property, though it lacks a pool, which may be a disadvantage in the summer.

✉ Triq Schreiber, Paceville ☎ 21382232; www.hotelvalentina.com
🚌 62, 64–68, 70, 164, 667, 671 from Valletta; 627 from Buġibba; 645, 652 from Sliema

SLIEMA
Hotel Fortina Spa Resort (€€€)
Sophisticated spa resort offering an all-inclusive package with daily spa treatments. The hotel has seven swimming pools and seven restaurants. Main garden area and pool for adults only.

✉ Tigne seafront ☎ 23460000; www.hotelfortina.com 🚌 63, 65 from Valletta to Sliema ferries; 62–64, 66–68, 622, 671 from Valletta; 70, 627, 662 from Buġibba; 645 from Ċirkewwa, 65 from Mdina/Rabat; 652 from Golden Bay

Park Hotel (€€)
A chic, six-storey hotel with modern art and fake marble giving a swank look to the lobby. Restaurant, café, indoor pool, sauna and fitness room. Child-friendly; half board available.

✉ Graham Street ☎ 21343780; www.parkhotel.com.mt 🚌 63, 65 from Valletta to Sliema ferries; 62–64, 66–68, 622, 671 from Valletta; 70, 627, 662 from Buġibba; 65 from Mdina/Rabat; 645 from Ċirkewwa; 652 from Golden Bay

Sliema Hotel (€)
A smart modern hotel with a café that opens out onto the pavement. Rooms with a view of the sea cost more and a range of family rooms are also available.

✉ 59 The Strand ☎ 21324886; www.sliemahotel.com 🚌 63, 65 from Valletta to Sliema ferries; 62–64, 66–68, 622, 671 from Valletta; 70, 627, 662 from Buġibba; 645 from Ċirkewwa; 65 from Mdina/Rabat; 652 from Golden Bay

Waterfront Hotel (€€)
A reliable, modern, clean hotel on the Sliema strip, the Waterfront makes a good mid-range choice if you want a full-service hotel option. There's a pool and sun deck on the roof with excellent views down the coastal inlet.

✉ The Strand, Gżira ☎ 21333434; www.waterfronthotelmalta.com 🚌 63, 65 from Valletta to Sliema ferries; 62–64, 66–68, 622, 671 from Valletta; 70, 627, 662 from Buġibba; 645 from Ċirkewwa; 65 from Mdina/Rabat; 652 from Golden Bay

RESTAURANTS

ATTARD
Villa Corinthia Restaurant (€€€)
The main restaurant of the Corinthia Palace Hotel and one of the best in Malta. The setting is superb. The whole place is elegantly furnished and decorated in a grand style. European menu.
✉ Corinthia Palace Hotel, De Paule Avenue ☎ 21440801 ☀ Daily 7pm–10pm; Sun lunch 12:30–2:30 🚌 40

MDINA AND RABAT
Bacchus (€€)
Notwithstanding a dungeon-like atmosphere, this is one of the best places for a decent meal in Mdina. There are some tasty hors d'oeuvres, speciality fish dishes, soups, grills and pasta.
✉ Inguanez Street, Mdina ☎ 21454981 ☀ Daily 9–9 🚌 80, 81 from Valletta; 65 from Sliema

Butcher's Grill (€–€€)
There's more than a touch of Africa at Butcher's Grill, where the spices of Tanzania flavour many of the marinades and dishes. Of course the restaurant specializes in meats, but there are salads, pizzas and pasta on the menu.
✉ 5 The Saqqajja, Rabat ☎ 21454117 ☀ Daily noon–3, 6–11 🚌 80, 81, 83, 84 from Valletta; 86 from Buġibba; 65 from Sliema

Ciappetti Tea Rooms (€€)
Lovely courtyard setting with wooden tables and a simple short menu of salads, rolls and home-made cakes. There is an open-air terrace upstairs on the bastion.
✉ 5 St Agatha's Esplanade, Mdina ☎ 21459987 ☀ Daily 11–3:30, 7:30–11 🚌 80, 81 from Valletta; 65 from Sliema

De Mondion (€€€)
Mediterranean cuisine and starters like avocado pear in coriander and tarragon batter served with arugula and an olive tapenade.
✉ Xara Palace Hotel, Misrah il-Kunsill, Mdina ☎ 21450560 ☀ Mon–Sat 7:30pm–10:30pm 🚌 80, 84 from Valletta; 65 from Sliema

Fontanella Tea Garden (€)

Panoramic view from the tables of the battlements of Mdina. Only light meals but an excellent selection of home-made cakes such as lemon meringue and black forest gateau.

✉ 1 Bastion Street, Mdina ☎ 21454264 ⏰ Summer: daily 10–10; winter: daily 10–6 🚌 80, 81 from Valletta; 65 from Sliema

The Medina (€€€)

Inside an old Norman house, with a vine-laden courtyard for summer and a fire for winter. The food is French, with Italian and Maltese influences here and there. Can be quite romantic.

✉ 7 Holy Cross Street, Mdina ☎ 21454004 ⏰ Mon–Sat 7:30pm–10:30pm (closed public hols) 🚌 80, 81, 83, 84 from Valletta; 86 from Buġibba; 65 from Sliema

SB Grotto Tavern (€–€€)

Step down into this terrific little tavern serving some real surprises. Fondue and moules marinière on the menu and an above-average wine list.

✉ Parish Square, Rabat ☎ 21455138 ⏰ Daily 12–2:15, 7–10

MOSTA
Ta'Marija (€€)

Voted best restaurant on the island for Maltese cuisine for four years running up to 2008, this family-run establishment is the ideal place to try a few new dishes. It's a lovely rustic dining room and there's live traditional music every Friday year-round and Wednesdays April to November. Try the weekend buffet, but make sure you reserve a table.

✉ Constitution Street ☎ 21434444; www.tamarija.com ⏰ Daily 12–2:30, 6:30–10:30 🚌 43–45, 47, 48, 52, 56–59, 65, 86, 145, 153, 157–159, 427

ST JULIAN'S, PACEVILLE AND ST GEORGE'S BAY
Le Bistro (€€)

Le Bistro is worth keeping in mind as one of the very few 24-hour food and drink places of any quality on the island. For fine dining go down the marble staircase to Le Petillant (€€€).

✉ Radisson SAS Point Bay Resort, St George's Bay ☎ 21374894 🕐 24 hours 🚌 62, 64–68, 70, 164, 667, 671 from Valletta; 627 from Buġibba; 645, 652 from Sliema

Caffe Raffael (€–€€)

Pizzas, pasta, salads and kebabs in a lovely stone-built restaurant. Reserve an outdoor waterfront table. Deservedly busy.

✉ St George's Road, St Julian's ☎ 21332000 🕐 Daily 10–11 🚌 62, 64–68, 70, 164, 667, 671 from Valletta; 627 from Buġibba; 645, 652 from Sliema

Eastern Breeze (€€€)

Asian fusion at its best, this is a contender for the best restaurant in Malta. Everything works, from the service to the food to the Jacobsen-like cutlery, and the sizzling chocolate desert caps it all.

✉ Intercontinental Hotel, St George's Bay, St Julian's ☎ 21377600 🕐 Tue–Sat 7–11 🚌 62, 64–68, 70, 164, 667, 671 from Valletta; 627 from Buġibba; 645, 652 from Sliema

Peppino's (€€–€€€)

At lunchtime it's a wine bar, in the evening the top two floors have tables overlooking the bay and reservations are essential at weekends, especially for the top terrace, which has a superb view.

✉ 31 St George's Road, St Julian's ☎ 21373200 🕐 Mon–Sat 12–2:30, 7–11 🚌 62, 64–68, 70, 164, 667, 671 from Valletta; 627 from Buġibba; 645, 652 from Sliema

Piccolo Padre Pizzeria (€)

Situated below the Barracuda restaurant; as well as pizzas (try the pizzotto) there are pasta dishes and pleasant starters.

✉ 194 Main Street, St Julian's ☎ 21344875 🕐 Daily 6:30pm–11:30pm

Quadro (€€€)

Fine dining indoors or outside. Main courses like monkfish and cuttlefish with a potato tart cooked in the ink of the fish.

✉ Westin Dragonara Resort, St Julian's ☎ 21381000 🕐 Mon–Fri 12:30–2:30, 7:30–11:30, Sat–Sun 7:30–11:30 🚌 62, 64–68, 70, 164, 667, 671 from Valletta; 627 from Buġibba; 645, 652 from Sliema

Zest (€€€)

Far Eastern minimalist decor greets you at one of the most popular restaurants along the resort strip. The menu melds Chinese, Japanese and Thai dishes from excellent fresh sushi to hot Thai curry. There's a chill-out bar with terrace just adjacent, so you can extend your stay for post-dinner drinks.

✉ 12 St George's Road ☎ 21388000; www.hoteljuliani.com 🚌 62, 64–68, 70, 164, 667, 671 from Valletta; 627 from Buġibba; 645, 652 from Sliema

SLIEMA
La Cuccagna (€)

At the sea end of Amery Street, this quaint and cosy little place can be relied on for tasty home-made pizza and pasta dishes; the starters and desserts are good as well.

✉ 47 Amery Sreet ☎ 21346703 🕐 Tue–Sat 7–midnight

VITTORIOSA
Café Riche (€)

Easy to find, on the right just before entering Vittoriosa's Gate of Provence. Just snacks like toasted sandwiches, but this is the only place to enjoy a bite of food so close to Vittoriosa.

✉ Cospicua ☎ 21820989 🕐 Mon–Sat 10–4, Sun 10–1

SHOPPING

HANDICRAFTS, ART AND ANTIQUES
Empire Arts and Crafts Centre

This huge crafts emporium sells just about everything. The lace work, paintings, glass and ceramics take second place to the largest selection of jewellery in Malta.

✉ 20A/B St Agatha Street, Rabat ☎ 21453245 🕐 Mon– Sat 10–6 🚌 80, 81, 83, 84, 86

Galleria Cremona

Marco Cremona is a Maltese artist, born in 1951, who studied in Italy and London and worked as an art teacher before turning professional. His paintings have been exhibited in Europe and are usually impressions of Malta.

✉ 13 Museum Road, Rabat ☎ 99463315 (mobile);
www.galleriacremona.com ⏱ Summer: Mon–Sat 10–6 🚌 80, 81, 83, 84, 86

Greenhand Leathercraft

This little shop has two branches inside the city walls. The action in the workshop can be seen and, as well as leather goods, some lace and gifts are also on sale.

✉ 28 Villegaigon Street, Mdina ☎ 21454689 ⏱ Mon–Sat 10–6

Lin's Lace

Some of the small craft shops in Mdina keep irregular hours but Lin's Lace can be relied upon throughout the year for jewellery, crafts, local wine, pottery and garments. You'll find the shop in the lane that leads from near the cathedral to the Craft Centre.

✉ Triq Bieb, Mdina ☎ 21563022 ⏱ Mon–Sat 9:30–5

Mdina Glass

Decorative glass is made here in the traditional manner by hand and mouth; also etching and crystal cutting.

✉ Ta' Qali Craft Village, Ta' Qali ☎ 21415786; www.mdinaglass.net ⏱ Oct Mon–Fri 8–6, Sat 8–12:30, Sun 9–4 (Mar–Oct); Nov–Jun Mon–Fri 8–4, Sat 8–12:30 🚌 80 from Valletta or Rabat; 86 from Buġibba; 65 from Sliema

Phoenician Glassblowers

Even if no purchase is made, it is still interesting to watch the fascinating process of glass being mouth-blown and handmade.

✉ Ta' Qali Crafts Village, Hut 10 ☎ 21437041; www.phoenicianglass.com ⏱ Mon–Sat 9–4:30

Ta' Qali Craft Village

The site is a disused airfield from World War II and the crews' Nissen huts are now devoted to the business of retailing lace, glass and other crafts. Mdina Glass have their workshop here.

✉ Ta' Qali ☎ 22141111; www.taqali.com ⏱ The village itself has open access. Each individual artisan has it's own opening hours – generally core hours of Mon–Fri 9–4, Sat 9–12

OPEN-AIR MARKETS

Many towns in Malta have a local open-air market once or twice a week and they are worth visiting if you are in the area, but do not go out of your way to make a special trip. Good for seeing the locals out and about.

✉ Birkirkara, near the Church of St Helen ⏰ Wed, Fri 7am–11am

🚌 41, 40, 47, 49, 52, 55–57, 59, 71, 73, 78, 157, 169. 560 from Għargħur; 580 from Buġibba.

✉ Naxxar, 21st September Avenue ⏰ Thu 7am–11am 🚌 54–56, 65

✉ Vittoriosa, St Margherita Heights ⏰ Tue 7am–11am 🚌 1, 2, 4, 6

ENTERTAINMENT

BARS AND NIGHTCLUBS

Axis

Apart from the main dance floor, there is also the Freestyle club, which plays less frantic music and, up on the floor above, a small designer-style bar with a tiny dance space and salsa music setting the mood. Open every night through the summer.

✉ Triq San Gorg, St Julian's ☎ 21318078; www.axis.com.mt ⏰ Daily 9:30pm–4am in summer 🚌 62, 64–68, 70, 164, 667, 671 from Valletta; 627 from Buġibba; 645, 652 from Sliema

B.J.s

This pub has a soul. There is a small stage for bands, often very good, and usually a pleasant upbeat atmosphere despite the dark and smoky interior. Jazz evenings featured.

✉ Ball Street, Paceville, St Julian's ☎ 21337642 ⏰ Daily 7–late 🚌 62, 64–68, 70, 164, 667, 671 from Valletta; 627 from Buġibba; 645, 652 from Sliema

Bar Native

This pub in Paceville does not encourage the under-25s and the music is not so loud that you cannot hear yourself speak. Wine by the glass or bottle and six types of draught beer.

✉ St George's Road, Santa Rita Steps, Paceville ☎ 21380635 ⏰ Daily 11–late (winter 6:30–late)

TRIPS AND SHOWS, CASINOS AND CRUISES

Casinos

The Dragonara Casino Barrière, Malta's original casino, has a bar and restaurant and a dress code – jacket and tie must be worn. The Oracle Casino (➤ 168) is more geared towards tourists. Several bars and restaurants, and the dress code here is smart/casual, with no shorts after 8pm.

✉ Dragonara Casino, St Julian's ☎ 21382362; www.dragonara.com
🕐 Mon–Thu 10am–6am, Fri–Sun 24 hours 🚌 62, 64–68, 70, 164, 667, 671 from Valletta; 627 from Buġibba; 645, 652 from Sliema. Free transport from Sliema and St Julian's

Cruises

Captain Morgan is a well-established tour company offering harbour cruises that depart from Sliema daily from 10:30am, and a daily day-long cruise around Malta and the island of Comino; a Blue Lagoon cruise, sunset cruise, overnight cruise; a Party Boat that departs Sliema at 7:30pm and an underwater safari (➤ 73). Also trips by Luzzo Cruises from Marsaskala.

✉ Captain Morgan Cruises, Dolphin Court, Tigne Seafront, Sliema
☎ 23463333; www.captainmorgan.com.mt 🚌 60–64, 67, 68 from Valletta; 70, 86 from Buġibba; 65, 86 from Rabat; 645 from Ċirkewwa; 652 from Golden Bay ⛴ Valletta-Sliema ferry (☎ 23463333)

The Mdina Experience

An audio-visual, multilingual spectacular spanning some 3,000 years of Mdina's history in half an hour. The 30-minute programme runs continuously every half an hour during the opening times.

✉ 7 Mesquita Square, Mdina ☎ 21454322; www.themdinaexperience.com
🕐 Mon–Fri 10:30–4 🚌 80, 83, 86 from Valletta; 65 from Sliema

Bay Arena

This multi-purpose hall holds concerts, gala evenings, product launches and Malta's largest New Year's party. There's an eclectic mix on the programme so consult the Tourist Authority about what's on during your stay.

✉ InterContinental Hotel, St George's Bay ☎ 23765767

The North

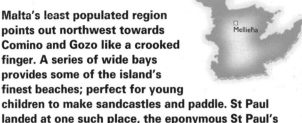

Mellieħa

Malta's least populated region points out northwest towards Comino and Gozo like a crooked finger. A series of wide bays provides some of the island's finest beaches; perfect for young children to make sandcastles and paddle. St Paul landed at one such place, the eponymous St Paul's Bay, when he was shipwrecked on a journey to Rome.

A series of high ridges makes this one of the most undulating parts of Malta, though the landscape isn't the most compelling reason to visit. Fascinating churches and ancient temples are found around every corner. Buġibba is the place for bars and nightlife, while the lower-key resorts are the perfect choice for a spot of gentle R&R.

BUĠIBBA

See page 160 (Qawra and Buġibba).

GĦAJN TUFFIEĦA AND GOLDEN BAY

The two sandy beaches of Għajn Tuffieħa and Golden Bay,
separated by a small headland, have military associations. It was
in Għajn Tuffieħa that the Turkish fleet gathered before beginning
the Great Siege of 1565, and the British trained their naval forces
in both bays during World War II. In 2008 the Maltese created
their first national park, **Il-Majjistral Nature and History Park,**
protecting the moorland and coastal landscapes between Golden

Bay and Anchor Bay. This encapsulates a good cross section of the island's natural environments – with numerous low-growing plants like golden samphire and Maltese spurge. Human activity, including farming, is evident, though this will be managed into the future. Within the park there are several historical and archaeological sites, including beehive tombs, carts ruts and ancient quarries. Later remains include those of a defence system built by the Knights of St John as late as the early 18th century.

✚ D2
Il-Majjistral Nature and History Park
⊠ National Park Office: 133 Melita Street, Valletta ⏱ Open access
✋ Free 🍴 Golden Sands Hotel (€–€€) 🚌 47 from Valletta; 652 from Sliema

MANIKATA

This small rural village is home to the most modern parish church on the island, which has received international acclaim. The Church of St Joseph was designed by Maltese architect Richard England to emulate the form of the ancient temples of Malta and was consecrated in 1974. Its lines offer an interesting contrast to the rich Renaissance and baroque of the other churches on the island.

✚ E1 ⊠ Golden Bay ⏱ Church: Mon–Sat 8–12:30, 4–7 🚌 47

MELLIEĦA

Mellieħa's popular sandy beach – the largest in Malta – is 2km (1.2 miles) north of town. It attracted Turkish pirates, and as a result the village of Mellieħa, which is set on a spur, was deserted in the mid-16th century. The town's present shape goes back to the 19th century when the steep main street, where houses cling to the rock, was laid out. Selmun Palace, a prominent castle with adjoining chapel, that dominates the area from its position up on Marfa Ridge, was built in the mid-18th century by Domenica Cathias. It was once owned by a charitable foundation which aimed to ransom Christian slaves who had been taken to the Barbary Coast. It is now a hotel. The heritage prize, however, goes to an ancient Marian grotto below, near the parish church of Our Lady of Victories, which has been a place of worship for centuries. The fresco of the Virgin Mary above the altar is said to have been painted by St Luke. The spring water in the grotto is credited with medicinal powers. Mellieħa has always been a favourite with the Maltese, and is becoming popular with visitors.

✚ E1 ✉ 23km (14 miles) west of Valletta 🍽 A good choice (€–€€) of cafés and restaurants 🚌 43–45 (also 50 in summer) from Valletta; 48, 145 from Buġibba; 48, 167, 450, 645 from Ċirkewwa; 645 from Sliema

MĠARR

There are not many settlements in the southwest of Malta so the farming village of Mġarr (there is a harbour with the same name in Gozo) makes a useful stop for refreshments in the course of exploring this corner of the island. It is also very close to the prehistoric sites of Skorba and Ta'Ħaġrat (▶ 161). The town's Church of the Assumption, called the 'Egg Church', has an interesting story. In the 1930s the local priest asked the villagers to donate eggs, that could be sold for a building fund. The villagers also donated their labour, which explains why with no outside help the building work lasted from 1912 to 1946.

✚ E2 ✉ 16km (10 miles) northwest of Valletta ⏰ Church daily 6–11, 4–7
🍴 A good restaurant (€–€€) next to the church 🚌 47

QAWRA AND BUĠIBBA

If you are staying in either of these tourist areas – the promenade makes for a pleasant stroll between them – there are plenty of diversions including countless restaurants, shops, a number of bars and nightclubs, and a casino.

Buġibba is intensely British and UK holiday-makers will not feel homesick here. The heart of the town is in the lively Pjazza Tal-Bajja. There is no sandy beach at Buġibba but flat rocks invite sunbathing and sunbeds can be hired facing out to sea. Cruises depart from the quay next to Bognor Beach for Comino and the Blue Lagoon (▶ 183). St Paul's Bay is a short walk away to the west along the coastal road.

Qawra is more stylish and a bit quieter.
✚ G1 🍴 Plenty of cafés and restaurants (€–€€)
🚌 To Qawra: 59, 159, 449 from Valletta; 70, 652 from Sliema. To Buġibba: 49, 58, 59, 159, 499 from Valletta; 48, 167 from Ċirkewwa; 70 from Sliema; 627 from Sliema ferries; 427 from Marsaxlokk

ST PAUL'S BAY

This premier resort area stretches from Mistra Bay on the west side of St Paul's Bay down to the mouth of the bay via Xemxija and up through Buġibba to Qawra on the east side of St Paul's. The sun, good beaches, beautiful water and seaside fun atmosphere combine to make it a mass-market destination. The original village of St Paul's Bay covers the area between Għajn Razul and St Paul's Church, for the saint was shipwrecked here in AD60. The elegant church of St Paul was built where he lit a bonfire and threw a viper into it, thus miraculously

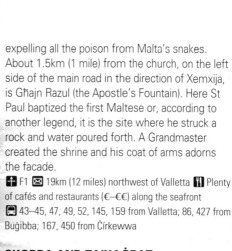

expelling all the poison from Malta's snakes. About 1.5km (1 mile) from the church, on the left side of the main road in the direction of Xemxija, is Għajn Razul (the Apostle's Fountain). Here St Paul baptized the first Maltese or, according to another legend, it is the site where he struck a rock and water poured forth. A Grandmaster created the shrine and his coat of arms adorns the facade.

🞤 F1 ✉ 19km (12 miles) northwest of Valletta 🍴 Plenty of cafés and restaurants (€–€€) along the seafront 🚌 43–45, 47, 49, 52, 145, 159 from Valletta; 86, 427 from Buġibba; 167, 450 from Ċirkewwa

SKORBA AND TA'ĦAĠRAT

These two archaeological sites may appear to be just a collection of old stones, but both have revealed important clues to Malta's prehistory. The Skorba site was excavated in the 1960s and the finds of pottery, animal bones and wheat make it likely that this was a neolithic and Bronze Age dwelling place.

The Ta'Ħaġrat site, in the centre of Mġarr, revealed evidence of temples that are contemporary with Ġgantija. This makes it the earliest standing temple site in Malta, and both sites, with Ġgantija (➤ 36–37), are the oldest standing monuments in the world.

🞤 E2 ✉ Skorba is signposted on the left before Żebbieħ on the road from Mġarr. Ta'Ħaġrat is a short walk from the centre of Mġarr 🕐 Ta'Ħaġrat: Tue 9:30am–11am (☎ 21239545). Skorba Temple: Tue 11:30–1 (☎ 21580590) 👋 Moderate 🍴 Good restaurant (€) in Mġarr near the church 🚌 47

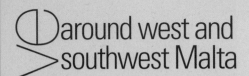

a drive around west and southwest Malta

This is a chance to explore another side of Malta.

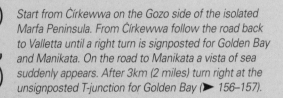

Start from Ċirkewwa on the Gozo side of the isolated Marfa Peninsula. From Ċirkewwa follow the road back to Valletta until a right turn is signposted for Golden Bay and Manikata. On the road to Manikata a vista of sea suddenly appears. After 3km (2 miles) turn right at the unsignposted T-junction for Golden Bay (➤ 156–157).

Detour to Golden Bay, a popular family beach. After a quick swim, sunbathe, or an exploration of the landscapes of the Il-Majjistral Nature and History Park (➤ 156–157), carry on.

After less than 1km (0.5 miles), at another T-junction, turn right and then straight on for Għajn Tuffieħa (➤ 156–157). Return to the main road and turn right, looking for a small sign on the right after 1.5km (1 mile) for the Roman Baths. After another 500m (550yds) a detour may be made to Mġarr (➤ 158–159).

See the 'Egg Church' (➤ 159), maybe stopping for lunch – the return journey is under 2km (1.2 miles). The main road leads to Żebbieħ and the Skorba Temples (➤ 161).

From Żebbieħ head for Mdina (➤ 118–125) and then follow the signs for the Dingli Cliffs (➤ 104–105). Turn left at the coast, keeping the Mediterranean on your right until the road swings inland. After 1.5km (1 mile) take the left turn at the roundabout, signposted for Rabat, and look for an unmarked crossroads with a church on the left. A left turn at this junction leads to Verdala Palace (➤ 109).

Stop for a tour of this cool palace if open.

Just 1km (0.5 miles) after the palace the first turn left leads to Buskett Gardens (➤ 103). A sign points the way to Clapham Junction (➤ 104).

Stretch your legs, and let yourself become absorbed in the mystery of the cart ruts. Then take the main road to Rabat.

Distance 20km (12.5 miles)
Time 4–6 hours depending on visits to places of interest
Start point Ċirkewwa ✚ B5
End point Rabat and Mdina ✚ F3
Lunch Bobbyland Bar and Restaurant (➤ 114) ✉ Dingli Cliffs

HOTELS

GOLDEN BAY
Radisson SAS Golden Bay Resort & Spa (€€€)
A lavish property of 337 luxury rooms set in pristine grounds, the Radisson is the best hotel in this part of the island. The spa and leisure complex, with glass walls looking out over the bay, offers a full range of facials and body treatments. There's an excellent water-sports centre on site and a choice of restaurants from casual to fine dining.
✉ Golden Bay ☎ 23561000; www.radissonsas.com 🚌 47 from Valletta; 652 from Sliema

MELLIEĦA
Luna Holiday Complex (€€)
Self-catering apartments in a modern complex with a pool, sun terrace, bar, restaurant, fitness room and mini-market and close to the beach. May to October and minimum three-day stay.
✉ Marfa Road, Mellieħa Bay ☎ 21521645;
www.lunaholidaycomplexmalta.com 🚌 43–45 from Valletta; 48, 145 from Buġibba; 145, 167, 450, 645 from Ċirkewwa; 645 from Sliema;

Mellieħa Holiday Centre (€–€€)
This Danish-run complex comprises 150 self-catering bungalows, each with two bedrooms, Olympic-sized swimming pool, restaurant, bar, playground and supermarket.
✉ Mellieħa Bay ☎ 21573900; www.mhc.com.mt 🚌 43

ST PAUL'S BAY, BUĠIBBA AND QAWRA
Primera (€)
Showing its age, a little, but still a comfortable abode in the heart of Buġibba and close to the sea and promenade. Most of the 80-plus rooms have small balconies and side views of the Mediterranean. A heated indoor pool, rooftop terrace and child-friendly.
✉ Pioneer Road, Buġibba ☎ 21573880; www.primerahotel.com 🚌 49, 58, 59, 159, 499 from Valletta; 48, 167 from Ċirkewwa; 70 from Sliema; 627 from Sliema ferries; 427 from Marsaxlokk

Sea View Hotel (€)

A small pool at the front of the hotel, suitable for children, with adjoining bar. Karaoke sessions twice a week, live music on Friday nights, pool table and internet service.

✉ Qawra Road ☎ 21573105; www.seaviewhotelmalta.com 🚌 59, 159, 449 from Valletta; 70, 652 from Sliema

Sol Suncrest Hotel (€€€)

With over 400 rooms this hotel has a good range of facilities including five restaurants, a disco, two lidos and two outdoor pools, tennis and squash courts, a health centre and a water sports centre. Facilities for people with disabilites are very good.

✉ Qawra Coast Road ☎ 21577101; www.suncresthotel.com 🚌 59, 159, 449 from Valletta; 70, 652 from Sliema

White Dolphin Residence (€)

Nearly 50 self-catering apartments located on the Qawra seafront. Most of the apartments have balconies overlooking the pool and Qawra Bay. Rooftop sun deck area with pool; children welcome.

✉ Qawra Road ☎ 21577485; www.whitedolphinmalta.com 🚌 59, 159, 449 from Valletta; 70, 652 from Sliema

RESTAURANTS

BUĠIBBA
Chez Gaetane (€€)

Always the subject of good reviews for its friendly service and value for money, Chez Gaetane is an excellent family option. Maltese and continental food.

✉ 79 St Anthony Street, Bay Square ☎ 21574453; www.chezgaetane.com
🕐 Daily 9am–midnight 🚌 49, 58, 59, 159, 499 from Valletta; 48, 167 from Ċirkewwa; 70 from Sliema; 627 from Sliema ferries; 427 from Marsaxlokk

MELLIEĦA
Alantil Boy Restaurant (€)

This family-run bar and restaurant serves snacks, grills, salads, burgers and a couple of Maltese dishes like rabbit and *bragioli* (rolled sliced beef filled with ham). Inexpensive and reliable.

✉ 61 Gorg Borg Oliver Street ☎ 21523533 ⏰ Daily 10–1am 🚌 43–45 from Valletta; 48, 145 from Buġibba; 48, 167, 450, 645 from Ċirkewwa; 645 from Sliema

The Arches (€€€)

Centrally located on the main street, The Arches restaurant has long been considered one of the best in Malta. It has a good wine list and the European cuisine is complemented by mouth-watering desserts.

✉ 113 Gorg Borg Oliver Street ☎ 21523460; www.thearchesmalta.com ⏰ Mon–Sat 7–10:30 🚌 43–45 from Valletta; 48, 145 from Buġibba and Ċirkewwa; 645 from Sliema; 167, 450, 645 from Ċirkewwa

Essence (€€€)

The silver service gourmet restaurant brings a touch of class to northern Malta. The menu is limited to a few well-chosen Mediterranean dishes such as Barbary duck breast or roast venison. Service is impeccable.

✉ Radisson SAS Golden Bay Resort & Spa, Golden Bay ☎ 23561000; www.radissonsas.com ⏰ Daily 7:30pm–10:30pm 🚌 47 from Valletta, 652 from Sliema

Giuseppi's Wine Bar (€€–€€€)

The menu changes according to the season so expect something fresh with the occasional surprise; the daily specials are good value and fresh fish is nearly always available.

✉ 25 St Helen Street ☎ 21574882 ⏰ Tue–Sun 7:30–11 🚌 43–45 from Valletta; 48, 145 from Buġibba; 645 from Sliema; 48, 167, 450, 645 from Ċirkewwa

Half Way Inn (€–€€)

As the name suggests, halfway down a hill between the village and the beach. Recommended for its generous portions, fresh fish and Maltese dishes. Popular with locals.

✉ Marfa Road, Mellieħa Bay ☎ 21521637 ⏰ Mon–Sat 6pm–midnight, Sun 12–2:30, 6–midnight 🚌 43–45 from Valletta; 48, 145 from Buġibba; 48,167, 450, 645, Ċirkewwa ; 645 from Sliema

ST PAUL'S BAY
Gillieru Restaurant (€€)
See page 58.

Nostalgia (€€–€€€)
The historic setting of a stone vaulted chamber is matched by the French and Italian cuisine at this atmospheric restaurant. The owner/chef ensures the highest standards.

✉ 14 Mosta Road ☎ 21576887 ⏰ Dinner: daily, lunch: Sun 🚌 43–45, 47, 49 from Valletta; 427 from Bugibba; 167, 450 from Ćirkewwa

Tarragon (€€–€€€)
A new fine dining option with Marvin Gauci, Malta's TV chef, in the kitchen has earned Tarragon five stars. The restaurant specializes in lava rock grilled meats, including excellent steaks in a selection of sauces; the vegetables are sourced locally for absolute freshness. The menu mainly concentrates on continental-style dishes.

✉ Church Street ☎ 21573759; www.tarragonmalta.com ⏰ Mon, Wed–Sat 7pm–11pm, Sun noon–3, 7–11. Closed Tue 🚌 43–45, 47, 49 from Valletta; 427 from Bugibba; 167, 450 from Ćirkewwa

SHOPPING

SOUVENIRS AND JEWELLERY
Aladdin's Cave
There are souvenirs galore plus gifts in this popular, inexpensive tourist shop. There are also knitted woollen garments – think winter at home, not here in the heat.

✉ 79 Triq ir-Rebbiengha, Bugibba ☎ 21573617 ⏰ Mon–Sat 10–9 (winter 10–7), Sun 10–4 (summer only) 🚌 49, 58, 59, 159, 499 from Valletta; 48, 167 from Ćirkewwa; 70 from Sliema; 627 from Sliema ferries; 427 from Marsaxlokk

J M Jewellers
You'll find a reasonable range of affordable jewellery in this well-positioned shop on the promenade. There is another jewellers a few doors down, so prices can be compared.

✉ 30 Islets Promenade, Buġibba ☎ 21583863 ⏰ Jun–Sep daily 9–10; closes early during winter 🚌 49, 58, 59, 159, 499 from Valletta; 48, 167 from Ċirkewwa; 70 from Sliema; 627 from Sliema ferries; 427 from Marsaxlokk

ENTERTAINMENT

BARS AND NIGHTCLUBS
The Amazonia Club
The Dolmen Resort Hotel hosts one of the most popular late-night dancing scenes with music from house to hip-hop to salsa.
✉ Dolmen Resort Hotel, Qawra ☎ 23552355; www.amazoniamalta.com
⏰ Daily 8pm–late 🚌 59, 159, 449 from Valletta; 70, 652 from Sliema

Buġibba-Qawra
The Buġibba-Qawra area attracts mostly tourists. Hotels like the Suncrest and the Ramla Bay Resort provide floor shows. There is also dancing and live music from country and western to karaoke.
Ramla Bay Resort
✉ Marfa, Mellieħa ☎ 22812281; www.ramlabayresort.com

Fuego Salsa Bar
The biggest club in the region with great Latin music and guest DJs. The large open terraces are heated during the winter. Join a dance class here if you want to emulate the professionals.
✉ Qawra Coast Road, Qawra ☎ 21386746; www.fuego.com.mt
⏰ Daily 4pm–1am 🚌 59, 159, 449 from Valletta; 70, 652 from Sliema

BINGO HALLS AND CASINOS
Fairplay Bingo
Bingo halls do not come any posher than this one, which is easy to find as it is situated opposite the Dolmen hotel in Qawra.
✉ Dolmen Street, Qawra Seafront, Qawra ☎ 21577677 ⏰ Daily 10–11

Oracle Casino
The casino has 11 gaming tables and 150 slot machines. There's a dress code after 8pm. Proof of identity and age may be required.
✉ Qawra Seafront, St Paul's Bay ☎ 21570057; www.oraclecasino.com
⏰ Sun–Thu 10am–4am, Fri–Sat 10am–6am

Gozo and Comino

Gozo is only 14km (9 miles) long by 7km (4 miles) wide, one third the size of Malta, but the island is no mere adjunct. The prehistoric stones of Ġgantija testify to its long history, and the mighty citadel at Victoria demonstrates how important it was to both the Arabs and the Romans.

Victoria

There is only one sandy beach on Gozo and no obvious resort areas, so visitors should not come expecting to find cosmopolitan distractions. The pace of life is slower in this agricultural and fishing community, which is the essence of Gozo's appeal. Fewer and smaller roads, less sense of congestion and a calmer atmosphere and superb swimming and diving combine to produce a place of escape and relaxation.

Tiny Comino, sandwiched between Gozo and Malta, draws daily visitors who come for the peace and quiet. Spring is the best time to visit, when the smell of wild thyme and cumin (after which the island is named) fills the air.

VICTORIA (RABAT)

Gozo's capital was called simply Rabat ('the town') until 1897 when a British Governor changed the name at the time of Queen Victoria's Diamond Jubilee, but the old name also remains in use.

The hilltop Citadel (Il-Kastell) is the focus of most visitors' interest and has a cathedral and museums. Victoria itself is a pleasant little town with a church worth seeing and a central square that buzzes with life in the morning before falling asleep during the afternoon. The central square, It-Tokk ('the meeting place'), has some tiny bars where you can sit and watch the gentle routine of Gozitan life, while a mysterious maze of narrow little streets and alleyways radiates out from the square.

✚ *Gozo c2*

ℹ️ Tigrija Palazz, Republic Street ☎ 21561419

The Citadel

The origins of this fortified enclave go back to Gozo's early history under Roman and Arab occupation. In 1551 Turkish raiders penetrated its defences and soon after this the Knights set about constructing sturdy bastions and ordering all Gozitans to spend their nights inside its walls – a policy that did not officially come to an end for almost 100 years. Now, the Citadel is virtually

uninhabited at night, though by day there is a constant flow of travellers visiting the cathedral, the few craft shops and museums.

The Cathedral Museum has church silver downstairs, ecclesiastical paintings upstairs and on the ground floor the bishop's 19th-century carriage, last used in 1975. The **Folklore Museum** is the favourite of many visitors with its down-to-earth collection of practical artefacts, including two splendid mills. The **Museum of Archaeology** has an important collection of Roman remains and Gozitan antiquities and, if time is limited, this and the Folklore Museum are the two worth seeing. An interesting exhibit is a 12th-century Arabic tombstone, inscribed in Kufic characters, mourning the premature death of a young Muslim girl. The **Natural Science Museum** has an unsurprising collection with the usual array of stuffed birds and geological exhibits. The Armoury is a disappointment because you can only peer through a gate at the exhibits. The Craft Centre has displays of local pottery, glass, wrought iron and lace, which are not for sale but may whet your shopping appetite for the goods in some of the small craft shops inside the Citadel.

Many of the buildings inside the Citadel were destroyed by Dragut, in the seige of 1551, and in an earthquake of 1693, but the whole complex has been sympathetically restored and a walk around the ramparts offers terrific views while evoking a sense of Gozo's ancient past.

Folklore Museum, Museum of Archaeology and Natural Science Museum

☎ 21562034 (Folklore Museum), 21556144 (Museum of Archaeology), 21556153 (Natural Science Museum) 🕐 Daily 9–5 💷 Inexpensive 🍽 Cafés and restaurants (€–€€) within walking distance

Gozo Cathedral

The entrance to the Citadel in Victoria leads into a piazza with broad steps occupying most of one side, which lead up to the cathedral dedicated to the Assumption of Our Lady. The exterior is perfectly proportioned, as befits a building designed by Lorenzo Gafà, but there is no dome where Gafà intended one. Visual compensation is provided inside: the flat roof has the illusion of a dome painted onto it, this *trompe l'oeil* being an outstanding feature.

www.gozocathedral.org.mt

✉ The Citadel ☎ 21556087 🕐 Museum: Mon–Sat 10–1, 1:30–4:30
✋ Inexpensive 🍴 Cafés and restaurants (€–€€) within walking distance

St George's Church

This lavishly decorated church, also known as the Basilica of St George, was built in 1678 after a design by Vittorio Cassar but has had many alterations since, including a new facade in the 19th century and the addition of a dome and aisles in the 20th century. You will find the interior richly adorned, with a wealth of baroque trappings earning it the name 'The Golden Basilica'. The altar has alabaster decorated columns supporting a canopy, a diminutive copy of Bernini's altar in St Peter's in Rome. Some interesting art work on display here includes a wooden statue of St George by Gozitan artist Paola Azzopardi, carved from a single tree. The altarpiece is by Mattia Preti and the vault paintings are by Giambattista Conti. The third Sunday in July celebrates the saint.

✉ St George's Square ☎ 21556377 🕐 Daily 4:30am–1pm, 3:30–7
✋ Free 🍴 Cafés and restaurants (€–€€) within walking distance

a walk around Gozo

For a walk in southern Gozo, drive or take a bus to Sannat, the most southerly village, close to the Ta'Ċenċ cliffs.

At the southern end of Sannat follow the signposted left turnings to Ta'Ċenċ/Dolmen/Cliffs. If driving, park where the last sign points left; next to an advert for Il-Girma restaurant.

You will find a fine view of Xewkija's domed church, the Rotunda (➤ 182), dominating the plain on your left. There is also a superb view of Victoria's acropolis, the Citadel.

You arrive at a crossroad of sorts (the roads have been surfaced) where you turn left, and not go straight on, which leads down to the sea and a small private beach belonging to the hotel.

The road you are on has a view of Comino and the western coastline of Malta up ahead in the distance, while all around is Gozo's barren landscape of limestone and scrubland. In this vicinity there are cart ruts (➤ 104) and neolithic burial mounds, but they are not signposted and it takes a bit of luck to stumble across them.

After less than 1km (0.5 miles) the road heads downhill for 600m (655yds); turn to the left and follow the road; after about 500m (550yds) the trail winds down to the inlet of Mġarr ix-Xini.

This is the perfect place for a rest and ideal for a picnic, and there is also the enticing prospect of a swim in the cool safe water.

From Mġarr ix-Xini it is 1.5km (1 mile) uphill along a surfaced road to a T-junction where the road to the right goes to Xewkija (▶ 182) and the left road is signposted to Victoria. (Along this road to the left there is a bus stop with a service that will take you back to Victoria.)

Distance 4km (2.5 miles)
Time 2 hours
Start point Sannat ✚ *Gozo c3* 🚌 50
End point Just north of Mġarr ix-Xini ✚ *Gozo d4* 🚌 42, 43
Lunch Chip and Dale Bar (€) ✉ Town Square, Victoria ☎ 21560506

More to see on Gozo

THE AZURE WINDOW AND THE FUNGUS ROCK

The natural phenomenon of Il-Qawra (Inland Sea) is a land-locked seawater pool but with a natural tunnel in the rock that allows the sea water in. A boat trip through the tunnel brings you to a door-like opening in the cliff through which you gaze at the Mediterranean. To Gozitans it has always been known as Tieqa Zerqa – the Azure Window – because of the colour of the dark blue sea. Nearby, off Dwejra Point, there is a rocky outcrop in the sea known as Fungus Rock.

✚ Gozo a2 ✉ 2km (1.2 miles) west of San Lawrenz 🍴 Drinks and snacks (€) available in the car park area 🚌 91 from Victoria

ĠGANTIJA TEMPLES

Best places to see, ➤ 36–37.

MARSALFORN

The fishing village of Marsalforn was popular with those Gozitans who could afford a summer break long before it was discovered by tourists. It is the island's only resort area but a fairly low-key one compared with somewhere like St Julian's or St Paul's in Malta. There are waterside restaurants, bars and hotels, boat trips, and water

activities can be arranged here.
Bicycles can be hired in the
village and, given the small size
of Gozo, this opens up a lot of
possibilities. A drawback to
Marsalforn is that there is not
much of a beach, but it is only a
short walk to the bays of Qbajjar
and Xwejni and here visitors will
have a bit more space.

✚ *Gozo c1* ✉ 4km (2.5 miles) north
of Victoria 🍴 Cafés and restaurants
(€–€€) on the quayside 🚌 21 from
Victoria

SANNAT

The village of Sannat, just south
of Victoria, has a reputation for
lace-making and boasts a fine
early 18th-century church, but
the best reason for coming
here is to begin a walk in the
neighbouring plateau of
Ta'Ċenċ. Gozo's top hotel
(➤ 184) is also located in
Ta'Ċenċ and to the east of it a
track leads to the small harbour
of Mġarr-ix-Xini. You could also
walk west of Sannat to Xlendi
via Munxar.

✚ *Gozo c3* ✉ 1.5km (1 mile) south
of Victoria 🍴 Il-Carruba Restaurant
(€€) in the Ta'Cenc Hotel (➤ 184)
🚌 50, 51 from Victoria

a drive around Gozo

The northern coast of Gozo can be breezy and was once desolate – a place of legends.

After disembarking at Mġarr follow the signposted road to the right for Nadur. The uphill road leads to a T-junction; take the right turn for Qala, less than 1km (0.5 miles) away. Exposed Qala has remnants of windmills, sun-baked dwellings and dusty roads with a Moorish feel. Continue straight past the church. Go left at the T-Junction, signposted for Nadur.

At Nadur the Kelinu Grima Maritime Museum exhibits sailing ships and battleships of World War II.

Leave Nadur on the road to Victoria and after 1.5km (1 mile) take the right turn at the junction for Xagħra. Follow the signs for Xagħra (▶ 181) and follow the road as it climbs uphill with a sign on the right for Ġgantija (▶ 36–37). Stay on the road to Xagħra after Ġgantija but take the second turning on the right, passing down the side of the church (cafés and bars in the square), and bear left at the signposted junctions for Marsalforn.

There is a good view of Marsalforn (▶ 176–177) as you enter the village through this backdoor approach. Stop here for lunch and a walk.

Take the road to Victoria from Marsalforn but turn right at the main junction before entering Victoria and look for the sign to Ta'Pinu (▶ 180–181).

The basilica at Ta'Pinu, a centre of pilgrimage for both Gozitans and Maltese, is noted for its mysterious voices and miraculous cures.

After the short detour to Ta'Pinu, return to the main road and take the signposted left turn for Dwejra. At St Lawrenz bear left in front of the church; the Azure Window is 1km/0.5 miles away (▶ 176).

Distance 12km (7.5 miles)
Time 2–5 hours depending on visits
Start point Mġarr ferry terminal ✚ Gozo d3
End point Dwejra ✚ Gozo a2
Lunch Il-Kartell (▶ 185)
The Kelinu Grima Maritime Museum
✉ Parish Priest Street, Nadur ☎ 21565226 🕒 Mon–Sat 9–4:45 (except public hols)

TA'PINU

This basilica, built between 1920 and 1931, hardly blends in with the surrounding countryside but is an impressive sight nonetheless. There was a chapel on the site from the 16th century, named after Pinu Gauci, who spent his time and money repairing it in the 1670s. At the end of the 19th century a local woman claimed to hear a voice in the church and gradually it acquired such a reputation for miracles that a bigger church was built around the original, which can still be seen inside behind the apse.

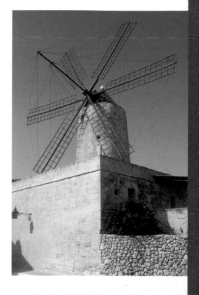

✚ *Gozo b2* ✉ 2.5km (1.5 miles)
northwest of Victoria ☎ 21556187;
www.tapinu.org 🎦 Mon–Sat
6:30am–12:15pm, 1:30pm–7pm;
Sun 5:45am–12:15pm, 1:30pm–7pm
❓ Multilingual information telephones
are available

XAGĦRA

The area around this small
town has a number of
archaeological sites, the
most famous of which is
Ġgantija (➤ 36–37), but
Xagħra is worth a visit in its
own right. The delightful
town square is home to the
attractive Church of the
Nativity and near by is Ta'Kola, an old windmill still in working
order. Also in Xagħra is a **Toy Museum** (➤ 73), and **Xerri's
Grotto** in Gnien Imrik Street is also open to the public. The
2km (1.2-mile) route from Xagħra to Calypso's Cave is well
signposted but the trip is sadly disappointing because a dark
hole in the cliff does not accord with anyone's idea of the
site of Odysseus' seven-year abode with Calypso. What is
worthwhile is the walk here from the east of Xagħra along
a footpath through the lush Ramla valley.

✚ *Gozo c2* ✉ 3km (2 miles) east of Victoria 🍴 Café (€), restaurant
🚌 64, 65 from Victoria

Toy Museum
☎ 21562489 🎦 Apr Thu–Sat 10–1; May to mid-Oct Mon–Sat 10–12,
3–6; Nov–Mar Sat and public hols 10–1 👋 Inexpensive
Xerri's Grotto
☎ 21560572 🎦 Daily 9–6 👋 Inexpensive

XEWKIJA

The people of this ancient village decided to build a larger church, now known as the Rotunda Church, and for the next 27 years money and labour from the villagers alone fed the construction of a massive edifice that is out of all proportion to the size of the village, and even to Gozo itself. The spectacular dome, which is only comparable to St Peter's in Rome and St Paul's in London, is 75m (246ft) high and 28m (92ft) in diameter.

🚩 *Gozo c3* ✉ 2km (1.2 miles) southeast of Victoria

🍴 Nearest restaurants are in Victoria

🚌 42, 43 from Victoria

XLENDI

Xlendi was a little fishing village until discerning visitors in search of relaxation discovered the place. It is still a charming spot, with a child-friendly swimming area which can be supervised while enjoying a drink or a meal. There is a diving school, accommodation (➤ 184) and some neat little bars and restaurants facing the sea.

🚩 *Gozo b3* ✉ 3km (2 miles) southwest of Victoria 🍴 Cafés and restaurants (€–€€)

🚌 87 from Victoria

COMINO

Comino is a small – 2.5 by 2km (1.5- by 1.2-mile) – virtually uninhabited island sandwiched between Malta and Gozo. There are no cars or roads and only one hotel that opens for the summer. The island's history is unremarkable for it

seems only pirates were attracted to its coves, and in 1618 a promontory fort, Comino Tower, was built on Comino's west side.

Unless resident at the Comino Hotel (➤ 184), visitors come for a day trip to enjoy the crystal-clear turquoise water or slow walks in the fresh air along vehicle-free pathways (and it is impossible to get lost!). The whole island is a wildlife sanctuary but botanically, the island is not as interesting as might be hoped, and it is not easy to find the cumin plant (kemmuna) from which the island gets its name. If staying on the island, there are excellent diving possibilities and even daytrippers can enjoy snorkelling if they bring their own gear.

The only significant beach area is the Blue Lagoon, formed by a channel that separates sun-baked and barren Comino from the islet of Cominotto, and only the large number of bathers detracts from the intrinsic beauty of this lagoon with its fine white sand. It is essential to arrive on Comino as early as possible, especially if you want to enjoy the Blue Lagoon. Be sure to bring protective clothing, cold drinks and a picnic, although food and drinks are available at the hotel.

✚ *Gozo f4* 🍴 Comino Hotel (➤ 184) 🚢 From Malta and Gozo

HOTELS

COMINO

Comino Hotel (€€–€€€)

This 95-room/26-bungalow hotel is the gateway to Comino and offers a good standard of accommodation and facilities where you can relax after your explorations. There's a choice of several restaurants and excellent water sports on site.

✉ Comino Island ☎ 21529821; www.cominohotel.com

GOZO

Kempinski San Lawrenz Resort & Spa (€€€)

It is hard to beat the hideaway location of this five-star hotel; it seems to be camouflaged. Inside, all is splendid luxury and the restaurants are some of the best on the island.

✉ Triq il-Rokon, San Lawrenz ☎ 22110000; www.kempinski-gozo.com 🚌 91

Lantern Guesthouse (€)

A family-run B&B in the centre of town, with a small restaurant.

✉ Qbajjar Road, Marsalforn ☎ 21556285; www.gozo.com/lantern
🚌 21 from Victoria

St Patrick's Hotel (€€€)

One of the best hotels in Gozo. Most rooms have balconies with views of either the sea, the countryside or a courtyard and there is a restaurant, bar and water sports for guests' use.

✉ Xlendi ☎ 21562951; www.vjborg.com/stpatricks 🚌 87 from Victoria

Ta'Cenc Hotel & Spa (€€€)

A strong contender for the best hotel in Malta and Gozo. It is in a tremendous location, overlooking cliffs and sea. All 83 rooms are stylishly decorated and have a terrace or garden. Sporting facilities include tennis courts and swimming pools and there is a private rocky beach with its own restaurant/bar. The accommodation includes stone-built trulli bungalows with distictive beehive roofs.

✉ Sannat ☎ 21556819; www.vjborg.com/tacenc
🚌 52 from Victoria

RESTAURANTS

GOZO

Churchill (€€)

Overlooking the sea with tables by the water's edge. There is a separate evening menu.

✉ Marina Street, Xlendi ☎ 21555614 🕓 Daily 10–late

Il-Kartell (€€–€€€)

A lively waterside restaurant serving good fresh fish. A speciality is mixed seafood with cream but the restaurant makes it's own pasta and serves excellent braised rabbit.

✉ Main Street, Marsalforn ☎ 21556918; www.il-kartellrestaurant.com
🕓 Daily 12–2:30, 6:30–11 (closed weekdays Nov–Jan) 🚌 21 from Victoria

It-Tmun (€€–€€€)

See page 59.

It-Tmun Victoria (€€€)

Sister restaurant to the Xlendi operation, but a little more formal with a more European classical menu. There's an à la carte menu backed up with excellent daily specials and tasting menus. It's also a wine bar with a contemporary interior.

✉ Europe Street, Victoria ☎ 21566667; www.tmunvictoria.com
🕓 Mon–Wed, Fri–Sat, 6:30pm–10:30pm, Sun noon–2:30pm,
6:30pm–10:30pm. Closed Thu

Jeffrey's (€€)

A friendly restaurant, with a small open-air section at the back. The food is delicious, and while the menu follows what is locally available at the time, visitors may depend on fish, rabbit and pasta.

✉ 10 Triq il-Għarb ☎ 21561006 🕓 Mon–Sat 7–10; closed Nov–Mar

Ta'Frenc (€€–€€€)

A beautiful vaulted dining room in a renovated farmhouse with exquisite food and an excellent wine list.

✉ Ghajn Damma Street, Xagħra ☎ 21553888; www.tafrencrestaurant.com
🕓 Wed–Mon 12–2:30, 7–10:30

SHOPPING

HANDICRAFTS, ART AND ANTIQUES
Gozo Glass
The glass-making workshop is on show inside the shop, on the main road just outside Għarb on the road to Victoria. There is some beautiful glass here, and a visit is recommended.
✉ Triq il-Għarb, Gozo ☎ 21561974; www.gozoglass.com ⏰ Mon–Sat 9–6 (workshop closes at 3:30), Sun 10–4 🚌 2, 91

SHOPPING CENTRE
Arkadia Shopping Centre
This is the largest shopping centre on Gozo, with a department store, boutiques, shoe shops and fast-food outlet.
✉ Fortunato Mizzi (end of Republic Street) ☎ 22103000 ⏰ Mon–Sat 9–7

ENTERTAINMENT

BARS AND NIGHTCLUBS
Il-Kartell
There is a billiards table and, although there is only taped music, sitting on the balcony and sipping drinks in this picturesque fishing village is a pleasant way to spend an evening.
✉ Marsalforn waterfront ☎ 21556918 ⏰ 8:30pm–1am 🚌 21 from Victoria

La Grotta
This open-air nighclub is delightful. An amazing location, with the bar in a cave, and a separate pub two minutes away. Club Paradiso above La Grotta plays more mainstream pop sounds.
✉ Xlendi Road, Xlendi ☎ 21551149 ⏰ 11pm–6:30am 🚌 87 from Victoria

BOAT TRIPS
Half- and full-day pleasure trips depart from Mġarr harbour and cover Gozo, Comino and the Blue Lagoon. Fishing trips and water sports also available. There are meeting points for free transport at Xlendi and Marsalforn at 9:45am.
✉ Xlendi Pleasure Cruises ☎ 21559967 ⏰ Full day cruise: Tue, Thu, Sat 10:30am departure, returning 6pm; half-day cruise: daily departing at either 10:30am or 2:30pm 🚌 21 from Victoria for Marsalforn; 87 for Xlendi

Sight Locator Index

This index relates to the maps on the covers. We have given map references to the main sights of interest in the book. Grid references in italics indicate sights featured on the town plan of Valletta and the map of Gozo.

Index

Acknowledgements

The Automobile Association would like to thank the following photographers, companies and picture libraries for their assistance in the preparation of this book.

Abbreviations for the picture credits are as follows: (t) top; (b) bottom; (c) centre; (l) left; (r) right; (AA) AA World Travel Library

4l Senglea, AA/P Enticknap; **4c** St Catherine Tat-Torba, Qrendi, AA/P Enticknap; **4r** Ġgantija Temples, AA/P Enticknap; **5l** Golden Bay, AA/P Enticknap; **5c** Spinola Bay, AA/A Kouprianoff; **6/7** Senglea, AA/P Enticknap; **8/9** Marsaxlokk, AA/P Enticknap; **10cr** Rabat, AA/P Enticknap; **10bl** Valletta, AA/P Enticknap, **10br** Sliema, AA/A Kouprianoff; **10/11** Carmelite Church, Valletta, AA/A Kouprianoff; **11** Corpus Christi Festival, Rabat, AA/P Enticknap; **12** San Guiliano Restaurant, AA/P Enticknap; **13** Cheesecakes, AA/P Enticknap; **12/13** Giannin Restaurant, AA/P Enticknap; **14** Valletta market, AA/W Voysey; **15cr** Market bread stall, AA/P Enticknap; **15bl** Bugibba wine shop, AA/W Voysey; **15br** Victoria pub sign, AA/A Kouprianoff; **16cl** Valletta festa, AA/A Kouprianoff; **16br** Valletta, bread, AA/P Enticknap; **16/17t** The Beheading of St John the Baptist by Caravaggio, Museum of St John's Co-Cathedral, Valletta, AA/A Kouprianoff; **16/17c** Xewkija, AA/W Voysey; **17** Medina, AA/P Enticknap; **18tr** Ħaġar Qim, AA/P Enticknap; **18cl** Auberge de Castille, Valletta, AA/A Kouprianoff; **18cr** Lace, AA/W Voysey; **19** Grand Harbour, Valletta, AA/P Enticknap; **20/21** St Catherine Tat-Torba, Qrendi, AA/P Enticknap; **24** Mosta's Good Friday Procession, AA/D Vincent; **25** Fireworks, AA/M Lynch; **26** Luga Airport, AA/P Enticknap; **26/27** Ċirkewwa ferry, AA/D Vincent; **28** Mosta, AA/P Enticknap; **29** Sliema, AA/A Kouprianoff; **31** Auberge Italy, Valletta, AA/P Enticknap; **34/35** Ġgantija Temples, AA/P Enticknap; **36** Ġgantija Temples, AA/P Enticknap; **36/37** Ġgantija Temples AA/P Enticknap; **38** Fort St Angelo, Valletta, AA/P Enticknap; **38/39** Grand Harbour, Valletta, AA/A Kouprianoff; **40/41** Path to Ħaġar Qim, AA/P Enticknap; **41** Ħaġar Qim, AA/P Enticknap; **42/43** Hypogeum, © Matthew Mirabelli/Alamy; **44cl** Painting by Favray, Image by Daniel Cilia, courtesy of Heritage Malta; **44bl** Main stairs National Museum of Fine Arts, image by Daniel Cilia, courtesy of Heritage Malta; **44/45** Room inside National Museum of Fine Arts, image by Daniel Cilia, courtesy of Heritage Malta; **45** Painting by Preti, image by Daniel Cilia, courtesy of Heritage Malta; **46** Council Chamber, Palace of the Grandmasters, Valletta, AA/P Enticknap; **47t** Armoury, Palace of the Grandmasters, Valletta, AA/P Enticknap; **47b** Palace of the Grandmasters, Valletta, AA/P Enticknap; **48** St John's Co-Cathedral, Valletta, AA/P Enticknap; **48/49** St John's Co-Cathedral, Valletta, AA/P Enticknap; **50** St Agatha's Catacombs, Rabat, AA; **50/51** Church of St Paul, Rabat, AA/P Enticknap; **52** St Paul's Cathedral, Mdina, AA/A Kouprianoff; **52/53** St Paul's Cathedral, Mdina, AA/A Kouprianoff; **54** Tarxien Temples, AA/P Enticknap; **55** Tarxien Temples, AA/P Enticknap; **56/57** Golden Bay, AA/P Enticknap; **59** St Julian's, AA/P Enticknap; **60/61** Mosta Rotunda, AA/A Kouprianoff; **62/63** Marsaxlokk, AA/P Enticknap; **64/65** Armier Bay Beach, AA/A Kouprianoff; **66** Cisk beer, AA/A Kouprianoff; **66/67** Bottled cheese, AA/A Kouprianoff; **68/69** Mellieħa, AA/A Kouprianoff; **71** Paradise Bay, AA/P Enticknap; **73** Toy Museum, Valletta AA/A Kouprianoff; **74** Auberge de Castille, Valletta, AA/P Enticknap; **75** Valletta, AA/W Voysey; **77** Marsa Sports Club, AA/P Enticknap; **78/79** Spinola Bay, AA/A Kouprianoff; **81** Valletta, AA/P Enticknap; **82** Auberge de Castille et Leon, Valletta, AA/P Enticknap; **84** Bibliotheca, National Library, Wyn Voysey; **84/85** St Paul's Church, Valletta, AA/A Kouprianoff; **86** Wignacourt Tower, St Paul's Bay, AA/W Voysey; **87** Maglio Gardens, Valletta, AA/W Voysey; **88** Maglio Gardens, Valletta, AA/W Voysey; **88/89** Argotti Botanical Gardens, Valletta, AA/W Voysey; **90** Fort St Elmo, Wyn Voysey; **91** Church of Our Lady of Victories, Valletta, AA/P Enticknap; **92/93** Manoel Theatre, Valletta, AA/P Enticknap; **94t** National War Museum, Valletta, AA/A Kouprianoff; **94c** National War Museum, Valletta, AA/A Kouprianoff; **95** Sacra Infermeria, Valletta, AA W Voysey; **96** Upper Barrakka Gardens, Valletta, AA/P Enticknap; **101** Marsaxlokk, AA/P Enticknap; **102** Għar Dalam, AA/P Enticknap; **102/103** Blue Grotto, AA/P Enticknap; **104** Clapham Junction, AA/A Kouprianoff; **104/105** Dingli Cliffs, AA/W Voysey; **106/107** Marsaskala, AA/W Voysey; **107** Marsaxlokk, AA/P Enticknap; **108/109** Qrendi, AA/P Enticknap; **109** Seġġiewi, Wyn Voysey; **111** Church of St Philip, Żebbuġ, AA/P Enticknap; **112/113** Żejtun, Wyn Voysey; **117** San Anton, AA/W Voysey; **118/119** Mdina, AA/A Kouprianoff; **119** Saracenic arch of Greek Gate, Mdina, AA/W Voysey; **120** Museum of Roman Antiquities, Rabat, AA/W Voysey; **120/121** Palazzo Falson, Mdina, AA/P Enticknap; **122** St Paul's Church, Rabat, AA/P Enticknap; **122t** Church of St Paul catacombs, Rabat, AA/P Enticknap; **123b** Verdala Castle, Rabat, AA/W Voysey; **124** Mdina, AA/P Enticknap; **126** Vittoriosa Square, AA/A Kouprianoff; **127** Vittoriosa AA/W Voysey; **128/129** Grand Harbour, Valletta, AA/P Enticknap; **129** Maritime Museum, Vittoriosa, AA/A Kouprianoff; **130/131** Vittoriosa, AA/A Kouprianoff; **132/133** Vittoriosa, AA/W Voysey; **134/135** San Anton Gardens, Attard, AA/A Kouprianoff; **136/137** Manoel Island, AA/P Enticknap; **138** Mosta Rotunda, AA/A Kouprianoff; **139** Ta'Xbiex, AA/P Enticknap; **140/141** St George's Bay, AA/A Kouprianoff; **142/143** Senglea, AA/P Enticknap; **144/145** Mellieħa Bay, AA/P Enticknap; **55** Għajn Tuffieħa, AA/P Enticknap; **156/157** Għajn Tuffieħa beach, AA/A Kouprianoff; **158** Mellieħa Bay, AA/P Enticknap; **158/159** Mġarr, AA/A Kouprianoff; **160/161** St Paul's Bay, AA/W Voysey; **163** Dingli Cliffs, AA/A Kouprianoff; **169** Xlendi, AA/W Voysey; **170/171** Roman mosaic, Victoria (Rabat), AA/P Enticknap; **172** Victoria Cathedral, AA/P Enticknap; **173** St George's Basilica, Victoria, AA/A Kouprianoff; **175** Xewkija, AA/A Kouprianoff; **176/177** Azure Window, AA/A Kouprianoff; **178** Xagħra Ramla Valley, AA/A Kouprianoff; **180/181** Ta'Pinu Church, AA/A Kouprianoff; **181** Ta' Kola Windmill Museum, Xagħra, AA/A Kouprianoff; **182** Xlendi, AA/W Voysey; **183** Blue Grotto Caves, Comino, AA/P Enticknap

Every effort has been made to trace the copyright holders, and we apologise in advance for any accidental errors. We would be happy to apply the corrections in the following edition of this publication.